DIPLOMACY
FOR THE
FUTURE

The Institute for the Study of Diplomacy concentrates on the processes of conducting foreign relations abroad, in the belief that studies of diplomatic operations are useful means to teach or improve diplomatic skills and to broaden public understanding of diplomacy. Working closely with the academic program of the Georgetown University School of Foreign Service, the Institute conducts a program of publication, teaching, research, conferences and lectures. An associates program enables experienced practitioners of international relations to conduct individual research while sharing their firsthand experience with the university community. Special programs include the junior fellowships in diplomacy, the Dean and Virginia Rusk midcareer fellowship, the Edward Weintal journalism prize, the Jit Trainor diplomacy award, and the Martin F. Herz monograph prize.

DIPLOMACY
FOR THE
FUTURE

Edited by
George C. McGhee

UNIVERSITY
PRESS OF
AMERICA

LANHAM • NEW YORK • LONDON

INSTITUTE FOR THE
STUDY OF DIPLOMACY

GEORGETOWN UNIVERSITY

University Press of America,® Inc.

4720 Boston Way
Lanham, MD 20706

3 Henrietta Street
London WC2E 8LU England

Printed in the United States of America

Co-published by arrangement with
The Institute for the Study of Diplomacy,
Georgetown University

Library of Congress Cataloging-in-Publication Data

Diplomacy for the future.

Essays based on proceedings of a conference held
in November 1985 at Georgetown University, sponsored
by the Institute for the Study of Diplomacy.
   1. United States—Foreign relations—1981-   —
Congresses. 2. Diplomacy—Congresses. I. McGhee,
George Crews, 1912-   . II. Georgetown University.
Institute for the Study of Diplomacy.
JX1417.D56   1987   327.2   87-3455
ISBN: 0-8191-6487-9 (alk. paper)
ISBN: 0-8191-6488-7 (pbk. : alk. paper)

All University Press of America books are produced on acid-free
paper which exceeds the minimum standards set by the National
Historical Publications and Records Commission.

CONTENTS

FOREWORD
David D. Newsom

I N A TIME of serious international tension, diplomacy, the means by which nations conduct business with each other, becomes critically important.

In November 1985, on the eve of the first Reagan-Gorbachev summit, a group of observers and practitioners of diplomacy gathered under the sponsorship of the Institute for the Study of Diplomacy at Georgetown University. Through the initiative of George C. McGhee, former under secretary of state and ambassador to Turkey and the Federal Republic of Germany, the day-long conference examined the present obstacles to effective diplomacy and took a look into the future.

This volume assembles essays based on the remarks of twelve of the participants, including Americans and non-Americans, statesmen, diplomats, scholars, and journalists.

Their observations raise serious questions.

Why has the United States not signed a major diplomatic agreement since 1979, despite numerous critical issues facing it in the world?

Is the United States capable today of dealing through diplomacy with the issues of an international scene far more complex than at the end of World War II?

Are the traditional conventions of diplomacy by which nations have for centuries communicated with each other now outmoded?

Do the executive-congressional confrontations on foreign policy frustrate effective U.S. diplomacy?

Do we know how to deal with the Russians?

In the light of closer European integration, have the patterns of Western diplomacy changed?

Is the professional Foreign Service of the United States adequate to its task today?

Have the media assumed a role of greater influence over the conduct of foreign relations?

The conference and this volume are part of the publications program of the Institute, which is supported, in part, by a grant from the J. Howard Pew Freedom Trust. Editorial assistance on this project was provided by Carol Clark.

DIPLOMACY
FOR THE
FUTURE

THE STATE OF DIPLOMACY

George C. McGhee

Diplomacy has been made more difficult by structural changes in the world environment: the demise of colonialism, the widespread decentralization of power once held by Europe and the United States, and the increased use of local aggression and terrorism as political tools.

A S A FORMER ambassador, I hold a strong belief in the importance of effective diplomacy in improving relations between nations. The conference that formed the basis of this volume grew out of that belief and a deep concern that diplomacy is, today, being seriously neglected. We do not intend either to praise diplomacy or to bury it, but to revive it.

Diplomacy might be defined in its most general sense as the application of human reason to resolving conflicts between nations. We believe that diplomacy can be an effective instrument, but that in recent years it has not been. We want to find out why this has happened.

I use the word diplomacy here in its broad sense. I do not wish to confine it just to ambassadors making speeches or giving dinner parties or negotiating treaties. I would define it to include all negotiations and exchanges of information and views across national borders, whether in the private or public sector, for the purpose of lessening tensions and effecting international agreements. Most of this effort is conducted quietly between foreign offices through their embassies. This is supplemented by actions taken in multilateral organizations, in international meetings, both private and public, and increasingly by public addresses and the media.

Some of us remember the period after World War II, which in many ways represented the golden age of diplomacy. Drawn together by the Nazi threat, the Allies were able to resolve their differences sufficiently to win the war and to organize a peace. When communist subversion threatened a devastated Europe, the United States took the lead in carrying out the Marshall Plan. When there was a threat of communist aggression against Western Europe, the Western allies organized NATO as a defense alliance. There were many other achievements: the financial agreements of Bretton Woods in 1944; the preservation of Greece and Turkey from a communist threat through the Truman Doctrine and Greek-Turkish aid in 1947; Ralph Bunche's mediation in behalf of the United Nations for a cease-fire in the 1948 Arab-Israeli War; the defense of Berlin against the 1948 Soviet blockade; the Tripartite Declaration of 1950; the Japanese Peace Treaty, and the Austrian Treaty of 1955.

There have also been, in recent years, other successful diplomatic efforts. I cite President Nixon's creation of SALT I, the establishment of relations with China in 1972, and the separation of Arab-Israeli forces in 1974. After a lull under President Ford, President Carter negotiated in 1978 the Camp David Agreement and the Panama Canal Treaty, and in 1979 SALT II.

With this background, I was startled one day to realize that the United States has not successfully negotiated an important international agreement in the eight years since, and none during the present administration. Indeed, had this administration been in office then, it would not have approved the Panama Canal Treaty. The Camp David Agreement, which was considered at the time a great diplomatic achievement, has been found to be flawed by a misunderstanding over the Israeli commitment regarding the West Bank. Unfortunately, the SALT II Treaty was never ratified.

This lack of diplomatic success is not limited only to our own country. During this same eight-year period, there has been a startling decline in the ability of other governments to settle their differences through negotiation and agreement. This applies not only to differences between communist and anticommunist countries, but also among members of the Free World. In many ways we have all regressed from previous agreements, and some have been disavowed. The United States has even watered down its commitment to participate in the World Court. During this period, local wars have proliferated and tensions have arisen that may lead to more wars. Relations between the United States and the Soviet Union have worsened.

Open denunciation and threats between nations, confrontation, unilateral action, and invasion without negotiation have become the order of the day. In 1980, Iraq invaded Iran without warning over the control of the Shatt-Al-Arab waterway and various Kurdish provocations. At this writing, neither country is making a serious effort to negotiate, despite U.N. offers of help and despite the disastrous effects the war has had on both countries. The United Kingdom and Argentina had ample opportunity to solve their Falkland dispute before the Argentine invasion, but they made no serious effort. The affair dragged on year after year. When Secretary Haig tried to assist them, neither heeded what he was saying. We ourselves have made little effort to negotiate our differences with Nicaragua, against whom we are engaged in an undeclared war.

The Soviets made no effort to mediate with Afghanistan, but invaded on the pretext of helping the communist government, whose prime minister they immediately assassinated. Despite U.N. prodding, there is no prospect yet of peace in Afghanistan that will permit a Soviet withdrawal. Whether or not our occupation of Grenada was justified—in any event the American people seem very happy about the results there—the clear fact is that we made no effort to negotiate the issues involved.

In the Middle East, President Reagan's peace proposals in September 1982, which were sound and consistent with previous efforts that we had made there, were spurned by Israel and Syria, the principal parties concerned. We made no serious diplomatic effort to stop the Israeli invasion of Lebanon, which disrupted beyond repair the fragile fabric of that country. We did negotiate successfully the withdrawal of the PLO from Lebanon, but the value of these efforts was negated by the ensuing Christian-Shiite war. Secretary Shultz's attempt to obtain the withdrawal from Lebanon of Israeli and Syrian forces was blocked by Syria's failure to negotiate an agreement. Since then, we have stepped back from the leading role we had hitherto played in Middle East negotiations. Although we still are willing to engage in discussions, for the first time since 1948 we have no active proposal on the table. The recent initiative by King Hussein showed promise, but the obstinacy of the PLO and other grave obstacles remain.

We must first of all recognize that many of the problems diplomacy faces today stem from what might be called structural changes in the relationships among the nations of the world. We have seen the world become divided among communist and anticommunist and nonaligned nations, between the haves and have-nots, between democracies and dictatorships, and on the basis of religion, race, and color. We have observed the loss of influence in the Third World that was once provided by the Europeans in their colonial systems. Although no one wants to restore the colonial era, there has remained an unstable vacuum of power in much of the developing world.

We have also seen a decentralization of wealth and power in the world, accompanied by a decrease in American influence. At the same time there has been an increase in the number of democracies in the world and a growing economic interdependence among the nations of the world. There have also been, however, the unfortunate withdrawal of certain areas into religious and ideological isolation and the increasing use of terrorism to achieve political objectives.

Most of these changes are beyond our control. They are so fundamental that their solution must await drastic changes in the attitudes of the nations of the world toward each other. Our country has an important role to play in this process, but it will take a long time; meanwhile there are certain things that can be done to improve the day-to-day conduct of diplomacy.

First, we must recognize the importance of the diplomatic process which goes on within the United Nations and the many other multilateral institutions that have been created since World War II. They must continue and be strengthened. I would like also to emphasize the importance of strengthening traditional bilateral diplomacy as a solution to existing problems, but more importantly as a preventive against new differences arising. The one most effective diplomatic method, I believe, is still the secret day-to-day bilateral flow of information between governments, accompanied by quiet discussions and negotiations. These result in better understanding of mutual interests and problems, leading to accommodation instead of conflict.

In recent years, these country-to-country points of contact appear to have been drying up. A *Wall Street Journal* article asserted the increasing irrelevance of ambassadors.[1] In some cases, according to the *Journal,* this is because they are incompetent political appointees; in others, because they are career diplomats not trusted by the president; or because the president and the secretary of state prefer to bypass ambassadors and negotiate through other channels. A recent U.S. ambassador to a major European country was rebuked by the host government for publicly criticizing a member of the cabinet.

We have, in the conduct of diplomacy, certain problems that are distinctively American. An obviously vital factor is the skill and the quality of our diplomats. We in America must create the incentives for our most talented young men and women to join the Foreign Service, and one of the ways we can do this is to offer them opportunities for eventual promotion, where deserved, to high posts. This assures that valuable training they receive as they develop will serve the interests of the country. It has always been accepted that we need a certain number of outstanding Americans from private life to

---

[1]Eduardo Lachica, "Lost Luster," *Wall Street Journal,* Aug. 29, 1984.

augment our career service—traditionally they have comprised about thirty percent. The injection of the prestige, experience, and leadership of these men and women has been invaluable.

In recent years, however, presidents from both parties have used ambassadorships flagrantly as a reward for campaign contributions and political services. The percentage of non-career ambassadors is now at an all-time high. Since David Bruce, who was one of our best ambassadors, half of our representatives in London have been successful businessmen who were heavy contributors to their party but knew little about Britain or the conduct of diplomacy. The same has been true for recent ambassadorial appointments to France. We still have delicate problems with Britain and France that require skillful handling. Our embassies in Paris and London are too valuable to our country to be put up for sale.

Another problem is in protecting our diplomacy against the demands of special interests. Policymakers must contend with the special pleading of countless trade, industry, financial, agricultural, and other groups. Recently, we have seen the disruptive effects of interventions into diplomacy by various religious groups, including the Moral Majority and other right-wing Christian organizations. The Reverend Jerry Falwell, in a critical juncture in the national debate on sanctions against South Africa, strongly urged support for the South African apartheid government, which our government has been urging to make meaningful concessions to the blacks. I am sure this must be confusing to most Christians.

Various U.S. ethnic groups are also attaining increasing influence over large sectors of our foreign relations: the Israeli lobby's influence over relations with Israel and the Arab states; the Greek lobby's effect on relations with Turkey; the Polish and other Eastern European lobbies' influence on relations with the Soviet Union; the Hispanic community's virtual monopoly over our immigration policy, and its strong influence on relations with South and Central America; and the influence of U.S. blacks on our policy with South Africa. These groups make increasingly large contributions to congressmen on key committees through their political action committees (PACs). Under the combined pressure of all of these groups, I ask you who in Congress is left to look after the American interest?

The power of the Israeli lobby, for example, has been the subject of a recent book, *They Dared to Speak Out,* by former Congressman Paul Findley.[2] Findley was narrowly defeated by an opponent backed by the American Israel Public Affairs Committee (AIPAC), which he says now contributes $3 million a year to congressmen, in addition to $4.5 million contributed by seventy-five other Israeli-oriented PACs. Congressman Findley calls the AIPAC "the preeminent power in Washington lobbying," which "has effectively gained control of virtually all of Capitol Hill's actions on Middle East policy." Findley says that this has been accomplished in part by creating a fear of retaliation and a resulting "dangerous erosion of free speech" in America.

The results of this speak for themselves. Seventy-four senators recently signed a statement opposing arms aid to King Hussein of Jordan, on whom the administration is relying in its current Middle East peace efforts, before President Reagan submitted his request to Congress. Israel is scheduled to receive this year (1986) $3.8 billion in aid of all types; however, Israeli congressional supporters are seeking $531 million more not requested by the administration.

Our annual aid to Egypt under Camp David, which is now about $2.3 billion, combined with that to Israel, currently takes forty percent of our total $15 billion foreign aid budget even though these two countries together comprise only one percent of the population of the world. This discrepancy reduces our aid to countries in the developing world, endangering our future relationship with them; we can no longer extend the type of economic development assistance that they badly need. Lobbying by the Greek minority led Congress to impose an arms embargo from 1974 to 1978 against Turkey,

---

[2]Paul Findley, *They Dared to Speak Out* (Westport, CT: Lawrence Hill, 1985).

our only NATO ally in the Middle East. The Turkish army is by far the largest military force in the Middle East and would play the major role in the event of Soviet aggression in this area.

The time has come for America to regain control over its foreign policy decision-making process from its own ethnic minorities. Our presidents must be free to direct our efforts toward achieving our own national interests. Indeed, we should tighten up our laws that regulate political contributions by all special interests. I believe the government should finance congressional elections in the same way we pay for presidential elections.

We must also, in the general conduct of our foreign affairs, make every effort to minimize the intrusion of domestic politics where this is done clearly for partisan advantage. The harassment by Senator Helms of the actions of the Senate Foreign Relations Committee in considering presidential nominees to ambassadorial posts through the abuse of senatorial privilege has badly handicapped the conduct of American diplomacy for several years.

We must prevent extremists from either the left or the right from gaining control of our foreign policy process. There is unfortunately a tendency on the part of such individuals to vie with one another in proving who can be the toughest. Those from both political parties with more moderate and objective views are in a much better position to represent our country as a whole. They are in a better position to work out the necessary internal compromises required in a democracy. Being in the center, they can develop much better contacts with each other.

Strobe Talbott, in his book *Deadly Gambits,* attributes the recent impediments in the development of a U.S. arms control policy to clashes among extremists within the administration.[3] He cites two assistant secretaries whose rivalry seemed to dominate and block the entire negotiating process. Many

---

[3]Strobe Talbott, *Deadly Gambits: The Reagan Administration and the Stalemate in Nuclear Arms Control* (New York: Alfred A. Knopf, 1984), p. 15.

participants, Talbott says, were against any concessions to the Soviets, some against any agreement at all.

The tendency of governments around the world to inject ideological considerations into the conduct of diplomacy unfortunately has resulted in the reemergence of situations that one might compare to the "holy wars" of centuries ago. The most obvious examples are the strong communist lines emanating from Moscow and other communist capitals, and the extreme Islamic policy pursued by the Ayatollah Khomeini in Iran. Unfortunately, President Reagan himself has injected such an element into our relations with the Soviet Union by his references to the "evil empire," to the Soviets being "cheats" and "liars." The resulting atmosphere precludes the possibility of successful diplomacy.

Negotiations between nations have come to be considered mainly as a way to win a victory, not to solve a problem. If we are going to get diplomacy back on track we must first "cool it." We must try to remove from diplomacy ideological extremism, political partisanship, and emotion. We must, ourselves, develop and take the lead in encouraging in the world more respect and tolerance for the rights and interests of other nations. We must be willing to negotiate with more flexibility—to give and take and compromise. There is, of course, the corollary that we must also be able to identify fundamental issues on which we cannot compromise. To accomplish this will require a better decision-making process within our government.

A successful businessman knows that in business it is better to bargain and make a deal, so he can go on to making other and bigger deals. This is the way business is conducted. A diplomat should try to negotiate the best arms deal he can; but he must understand that if he fails, the threat of nuclear war will continue and both sides will lose. The people of the world, both East and West, are tired of the present diplomatic impasse. They are demanding a reduction in the threat of nuclear war. This is why they are putting such great pressure on President Reagan and Chairman Gorbachev to "cut a deal," which is what diplomacy is all about.

2

A POLITICIAN LOOKS AT DIPLOMACY

Edmund S. Muskie

The diplomat is like a politician in seeking votes, not for himself but for the nation, also in seeking friends, balancing interests, occasionally twisting arms and trading off. This involves hard bargaining, talking, and compromising.

IS THERE A future for diplomacy?

We have many significant diplomatic accomplishments in our history, beginning with Benjamin Franklin's extraordinary role in gaining allies for our independence.

As a nation we can be proud, in more recent days, of that group of men and women that helped negotiate a return to order after World War II. One of them, the late Ellsworth Bunker, founded the Institute for the Study of Diplomacy. I succeed him as chairman of that Institute with a humble recognition of his great service to this country.

Currently, a significant diplomatic event is taking place in Geneva. There is no negotiation more difficult, nor more important for all of us, than that between the leaders of the United States and the Soviet Union. No matter what the party or the nation, people wish them success in reducing the deep chasm between these two powers.

In our country, the road to that summit was tortuous. There are those both in and out of government who clearly did not want to see the president sit down with the Russians. And that says something about attitudes toward diplomacy in the United States. Skepticism toward diplomacy is widespread in our society, particularly if it involves talking with our adversaries. The nature of today's problems and the alternatives, however, require us to talk.

I came to diplomacy from the world of politics. There are those who question whether politicians should be—or can be—diplomats. In his book, *Diplomacy,* Sir Harold Nicolson decried several aspects of the new "democratic diplomacy." He mentioned the ratification process, "the irresponsibility of the sovereign people,"[1] ignorance, delay, publicity and, with all these, "the tendency to allow their politicians to take a personal part in negotiation."[2]

The distance between the Senate Office Building and the State Department, is, in many ways, great. Yet, I found many similarities between these two worlds in the time given to me as secretary of state. As a politician, I felt at home as secretary of state. Diplomacy is somewhat like campaigning, but on a larger stage. The diplomat is seeking votes, not for himself or herself, but for the nation. The diplomat is doing what the politician does: seeking friends, balancing interests, occasionally twisting arms, occasionally trading off.

The Senate could not operate without the traditions of hard bargaining, talking, and compromising. The same is true of our relations with other nations. Talks with our adversaries can serve our interests—even when they do not produce agreements. They demonstrate to others our willingness to hear the other side; they can clarify the respective positions and often avoid serious misunderstandings regarding either substance or intentions.

During my term as secretary of state, I held two meetings with my Soviet counterpart, the veteran Andrei Gromyko. They were not easy, but each was useful. In the first, I made clear our strong opposition to the Soviet presence in Afghanistan. In the second meeting, we discussed the Iraq-Iran war. The Reagan administration has established a pattern of bilateral talks with the Russians on regional issues. The Soviets

---

[1] Sir Harold Nicolson, *Diplomacy* (Oxford University Press, Third Edition, 1964), p. 46.

[2] Ibid., p. 52.

are major players on the world stage; it is important that we talk to them.

There are those in this country who want us to try diplomacy only if we hold all the cards, only if the other fellow is so overwhelmed that he lays down his cards without a play. While some might like to, we do not play that way in our domestic politics; we cannot expect to do that on the world stage.

Perhaps, for a few years after the World War, the world was that way. We had a position of commanding power. Today there are many players with strong cards to play. There is no automatic majority for the United States. We must work for it in the world as a politician works for it at home.

When a candidate enters a political campaign, there are no assumptions. The territory is carefully surveyed because the interests and attitudes of each group are important. The good campaigner does not hesitate to wade into those parts of the constituency that may not, at least initially, be friendly. There is no other way to succeed. In my view, we must approach our relations with the rest of the world in the same way. We do not make it easy on ourselves to do so. A politician learns much in Foggy Bottom.

There are many players in our diplomatic arena. I fully understand why the diversity of national interests and the complexity of our bureaucracy make this so. A new player quickly learns that our diplomacy speaks with many voices. In a political campaign, you can fire the staff member that speaks out of line. A secretary of state does not have that luxury. Neither does an ambassador. Our diplomats must be skilled, not only in negotiating with others, but in explaining the often multiple versions of our policies.

The responsibilities in the executive branch are heavy. In the legislative branch, the issues are the same. Many are momentous and there is not one of us who has not agonized over this or that vote. The buck stops in the executive branch, however, and one is suddenly conscious that the issue is not just a vote but what the nation will do. Even in the short time I was there, I came to sympathize with Dean Rusk's complaint that foreign affairs never slept because one-half of the world was always awake.

Being in that position also makes one respectful of the difficult choices facing our diplomacy in any period. Seldom was an options paper brought to me that had an easy alternative. I was often struck, too, by the difficulty of determining the facts of a situation—despite our effective intelligence organization. Even if the facts were all there, people could disagree about their significance.

Each administration, and perhaps each new secretary of state, has entered office imagining or believing that there were in some areas alternative policies preferable to those followed by his predecessors. In some instances this is true; in many others, the new team quickly discovers that the limits of policy maneuvering are greater than had been believed. This happened with us in the Carter administration on such matters as Korea. It has certainly happened in the Reagan administration in such regions as the Middle East.

The politician is keenly aware of the public aspect of diplomacy. He or she quickly learns that much of the electorate is following foreign affairs with the same intensity with which they follow taxes and the budget. Today television has made international crises domestic crises; the drama of a Middle East hijacking comes as quickly and as clearly into every living room as a fire next door.

Therefore, our diplomacy today cannot be conducted without significant support by the electorate. I can tell you from experience that there is no greater sense of strength in diplomacy than being able to walk into an international meeting knowing that the Congress and the people of the United States are standing there with you. And there is no greater feeling of isolation than to realize that the support for your actions may not be there. The list, unfortunately, is long of those diplomatic actions we have attempted as a nation that have been repudiated by the Congress and the people.

I discovered that a strong degree of local support is necessary, not only because we need it at home, but also because others follow our politics very closely. They are as aware as we of issues about which the American public may be deeply divided.

I found that the other foreign ministers I met with were politicians, too. They were sensitive to the sentiment at home—to the survival of their government, their administration. They were limited, as politicians and diplomats are everywhere, by the realities of their political environment. They had constituents, too.

I came from the Congress. There are those who say the Congress is an obstacle to diplomacy. I acknowledge that it often complicates the task of relating to others. Ours is a complicated and complex nation, and the Congress reflects that. As a nation, we can go badly astray if our relations and agreements with others do not reflect the attitudes of the nation. Congress is a reflection of those attitudes, those fears, and those concerns.

Politics takes a special brand of courage. Candidates put their lives, their futures, their families on the line. Those who join with the candidate in a campaign share that risk. Diplomacy also requires courage—the courage to seek solutions to intractable problems, to challenge the conventional wisdom of policies, and to endure the criticism of those unsympathetic with the process or the outcome.

At this point, I would like to say a word about that fine group of professionals in the U.S. Foreign Service. There is, regrettably, a natural tension between the politician and the career government servant. They tend to look at issues from quite different perspectives. The Foreign Service has not always been well treated on the Hill. I found them a superb group; I could not have done my job without their loyal support. Some politicians perpetuate the myth that the Foreign Service cannot be loyal to one administration if they have served under another. This is nonsense. I found the Foreign Service officers to be of the highest caliber, dedicated professionals prepared to serve the policies of a president but, in the case of the more courageous ones, willing at the same time to challenge questionable assumptions and conventional wisdom and to point out the weaknesses of politically motivated assumptions at home. Bold steps can pay off in both politics and diplomacy, but often at great risk. Anwar Sadat's famous trip to Jerusalem was both a political and a diplomatic risk. It accomplished much, but at a tragic cost.

Jimmy Carter, for whom I worked all too short a time, was a man prepared to take both political and diplomatic risks. His record of diplomatic successes has rarely been equaled in a single term: Camp David, SALT II, the Panama Canal Treaty, and establishing relations with China. In the latter, he was building upon one of the successes of the Nixon administration in opening the door to the People's Republic. Yet, each of these diplomatic successes represented a serious, and potentially politically fatal, risk.

It is fair to reflect, nevertheless, how different our situations—as difficult as they are—would be in the Middle East, Central America, and East Asia if Egypt and Israel were still at war, if we were still facing the protests in Panama, and if we were still knocking on the door in China.

As the Carter years demonstrated, the results of diplomacy are far from clear cut. In the often polite realm of international diplomacy, it is not always possible to know exactly what others are thinking. There are no votes that can be counted to give a truly accurate view of the public or international mood. Diplomacy is at the mercy of opinion—an opinion often difficult to discern.

Whether or not diplomacy has been discarded as a national strategy, we have, I fear, lost some of our diplomatic momentum. Perhaps some of it will be recaptured in Geneva.

This is clearly not the time to speculate on what that outcome might be. I strongly believe that the centerpiece of our discussions with the Soviets must be arms control. I believe the world is a safer place today because we have the Limited Test Ban Treaty, the SALT I limits on offensive arms, the Anti-Ballistic Missile Treaty, and the SALT II Treaty. I do not believe in agreements for their own sake, but I believe we can negotiate agreements with the Soviets that are useful to us. We should not sell our diplomacy short in this area.

There are those who express surprise that the Soviet offers

are one-sided in their favor. We should not expect anything else. We do the same thing. We would be foolish if we did not. The job of the diplomat is to find a way to satisfy the legitimate needs of both sides. In the case of our arms control negotiations with the Soviets, I do not believe we can stand rigid on the nonresearch aspects of the Strategic Defense Initiative and still achieve an agreement.

The issues of the Third World will continue to challenge both the wisdom of our policymakers and the skills of our diplomats. We are again engaged in a national debate about the nature of these issues. The present administration sees them primarily as part of a global confrontation with the Soviets. In my view, this is a dangerously oversimplified approach. If we do not pay attention to the regional histories and the regional realities, and do not ask the hard questions about where policies are taking us, we can once more become bogged down in local wars. The proper task of the United States is to remain in a position in which we can play a role in resolving, not exacerbating, local disputes. I remain convinced that that is the only way to reduce the possibility of a further expansion of Soviet influence in southern Africa, Central America, and the Middle East.

During my time as secretary, I was impressed by the degree to which our influence is desired, occasionally even by those less friendly toward us. People look to us with respect and admiration and often with a surprising degree of trust. We should not toss that lightly aside by identifying ourselves with those who face the strong oppposition of their people.

It is not trite to say that we face some very difficult choices in today's world. The role of diplomacy in sorting out the correct paths and in working with others to make them possible is indispensable. We cannot as a nation be too proud or too afraid to sit with our adversaries and discuss the dangerous issues of today's world. We should have more confidence in our ability to deal with others. We who have an active, vibrant, and highly competitive political system seem apprehensive about using our political skills in the international arena.

A political candidate who loses momentum, loses. A nation that pulls back from an active role on the world's diplomatic stage also threatens a loss of interests and influence. We have too often seemed hesitant in our diplomacy. We have a fine candidate in the United States of America. We have a world that, by and large, looks favorably upon us and is often puzzled about how we handle our foreign relations.

It is time we showed the courage to make our diplomacy work. This requires not only the skill of our diplomats but also our close attention to the attitudes and concerns of our people. In our democracy, diplomacy and politics are inseparable. Democratic freedom and a deep sense of social responsibility as we know them are part of our conditioning. It comes from the good fortune of long tradition, of a new continent, and of those who had the intellectual and moral courage to oppose authority. They were rare at the time of our founding and are rare today. We cannot expect that they will be quickly or easily transferred to those formed in a very different society.

3

THE DOMESTIC ENVIRONMENT

Elliot L. Richardson

One problem affecting diplomacy lies in the State Department's considering itself to have departmental interests, coordinate with those of Treasury, Defense, and other agencies. In fact the department has no interests distinguishable from those of the president. Successful secretaries like Acheson and Dulles derived their influence from becoming and being perceived as alter egos of the president in the formulation and execution of foreign policy.

IN AN ATTEMPT to address a broad subject under the heading of the domestic environment of diplomacy, executive decision making and implementation, I will begin by considering briefly the increasingly interlocked and interdependent structure of the global system within which we live. This is almost a cliché, and because of that, new efforts of imagination are required to grasp the significance of what is happening. The failures of savings and loan associations in Ohio and Maryland visibly create tremors throughout the world financial system, and what can be said on that score could be multiplied through endless other examples. The increased volume of communications activities and trade transactions of all kinds from country to country is a phenomenon which in itself, I think, largely refutes the notion that diplomats and diplomatic missions have lost importance. It may be that in some of the traditional areas of bilateral relations others have been able, through electronics or transportation, to effect communications from government to government that do not directly engage the ambassador. Meanwhile, however, all these other transactions, which are, in many instances, of great instrinsic importance in themselves, have increased the responsibilities of our diplomatic missions.

The processes of economic, financial, commercial, and technological development and change are phenomena that spill across national boundaries. They have created the need for multilateral institutions—the greater effectiveness of those which we have and, in some instances, the creation of new ones. The role of transnational corporations and their place in the world is a subject of enormous importance, interest, and concern. There is also the question of how best to take advantage of their capacity to transfer capital and technology, to train people while holding them accountable both to their investors and to the countries where their activities take place. This is a problem that will require increasing thought and attention. The growing gap between the realities of global interdependence and the institutional capacity for dealing with these realities is perhaps demonstrated most sharply in the context of financial and economic relations. We see signs of an awareness of the need to deal afresh with these problems as well.

A consequence of all of this is that virtually every department and agency of the executive branch of the U.S. government and almost every committee and subcommittee of the Congress has legitimate interests and concerns about events that occur beyond our borders. This is quite obvious, of course, in the case of the departments of Defense, the Treasury, Commerce, Agriculture and, to a slightly lesser degree, the Department of Transportation. The Federal Communications Commission is concerned with matters involving international telecommunications, and the Labor Department with immigration matters and the pressures of labor to flow across national boundaries. Given these facts, these visible trends and their implications, one then has to consider the question of how the executive branch is organized to address them. Evidently, there is a need for the maximum feasible degree of coherence, consistency, and continuity in formulating and conducting policy. There is a need for the capacity to develop strategic approaches to dealing with the problems of the world and U.S. interests in the world.

Strategy needs to be perceived, first of all, in terms of its contribution to creating a sense of direction, determining how to get there from here, and affording the means of measuring progress. However, strategy has another and, in an increasingly complex society, a very different and equally important contribution, and that is as a framework for achieving communicability and intelligibility in formulating and conducting policy. The communication of a strategy can also serve as a means of engaging people in developing an understanding of the interests of the United States abroad. Through the involvement of their understanding and participation in formulating policy, there is then created the potential for building the necessary consensus without which there is no possibility of continuity and coherence.

How is it possible to achieve coherence, consistency, and continuity in the midst of this enormously complex set of concerns with such a large number of legitimate participants?

I may be one of the very few people around who harps continually on the significance of complexity as it has affected the conduct of the presidency, the role of the Congress, and, of course, the executive branch. The most dramatic demonstration of it is the multiplication of special subcommittees and the increase of congressional staff. I do not think that it is a manifestation merely of self-aggrandizement; it is an effort to cope with the reality that complexity increases as the product of other exponential trends interacting on each other. I will not elaborate on that, but I think it is a fact. One of its results is the increase in the paper flow; and the only ways you can deal with this are by attempting 1) to think strategically so that details fall into place, 2) to synthesize and to see the relevance of data in a larger picture, 3) to articulate goals which can in turn contribute to seeing coherent relationships and patterns, 4) to accept the necessity for addressing priorities at a given time, and, perhaps most importantly, 5) to accept the consequences of choice. We tend, as Americans, to want to have everything at once, to want to have it both ways, and to fail sometimes to think through the costs of choice. That failure, in turn, contributes to the multiplicity of communications because there is an assumption that everything can be addressed, and everything can be done at once, as if it were assumed that any individual could sample everything offered in a cafeteria. I think that it is only through the imposition of what are essentially intellectual disciplines that we can cope with complexity.

At an earlier stage, it was possible to achieve strategic direction and to introduce a kind of presiding intelligence into all this through the generally accepted assumption that the State Department had a kind of primacy in dealing with matters beyond the low water mark. Two things have affected that assumption, however. One has been the emergence of the degree of interest and concern of the other departments and agencies that I have already mentioned. The other is the tendency on the part of the State Department as an institution to think of itself as having departmental interests. In the transitional period between the Johnson and the Nixon administrations, it was a given that the State Department coordinated with Defense, Treasury, and the other departments. It was also assumed that the president needed a staff whose function was to distill a determination of the national interest of the United States in dealing with matters of national security and, hence, foreign policy.

If we made a mistake in that transition period in negotiating the charter of the National Security Council and its appendages, it was in our acceptance of that premise. This was not something that I understood at the time, however. It really is only in looking back and in later State Department experience, that I realized that there was another way of achieving coherence and consistency and providing the continuity that rests on consensus—and that is through denying the premise that the State Department has any interest distinguishable from the president and the United States. Looking back, it is quite clear that the success of a Dean Acheson or, perhaps, a John Foster Dulles, resulted from their ability to become and to be perceived as alter egos of the president in formulating and executing foreign policy. And, because they were the alter egos of the president, you never knew where the president's thinking reflected the influence and advice of his secretary of state or whether the secretary of state's utterances were expressions of views communicated to him by the president. In any case, because there was no seam in that aspect of the process, there could equally be none between the secretary of state and the Department of State, as the instrument through which data could be brought to bear upon the decision-making process and through which the policies determined upon could be carried out. There was a continuity of articulation between the brain and the arm and the finger that created the perception that these things were all of a piece.

We are at a point, I believe, where we need to think about how to recreate that kind of a relationship. I think it is fair to say that in the present administration Secretary Shultz and National Security Advisor Robert McFarlane worked together very well, so far as one could judge, and that there was a high degree of coherence in conducting policy as long as they were cooperating. There could be a longer-term contribution to the extent that diplomats think of themselves as participants in mediating and developing U.S. policy in ways that engage the other agencies or the other interests at stake. There is no reason for an American diplomat to deal with the Department of Agriculture or the Department of the Treasury as if somehow their perceptions of U.S. national interests were less important than those of the Department of State. To the extent that there are differences, such differences can be addressed through a process in which the State Department itself takes the lead. Such a process, in the long term, can work only to the extent not only that the department itself or a specially created interdepartmental group is charged with it, but also to the extent that each individual representative of the United States, each Foreign Service officer thinks of him or herself in this role.

The consequence, paradoxically, is to demonstrate that the only way to achieve a truly effective diplomacy in the conduct of U.S. relations with the rest of the world is to assume that the diplomat must also be a diplomat in conducting negotiations within the U.S. government. It is a commonplace, of course, that frequently the most difficult negotiations in which U.S. diplomats engage are those within the U.S. government. This has tended to be viewed as a drag on the process rather than as an integral and necessary function which the State Department and its diplomats embrace. For, after all, let us never forget that a diplomat of the United States abroad is not a Foreign Service officer, except by virtue of the status he or she occupies within a personnel system. He or she represents not the State Department, but the president of the United States. Graham Martin certainly never forgot that. It was Graham Martin, as ambassador to Thailand, who reminded Vice-President Hubert Humphrey that when the vice-president was in Thailand, he was outranked by the ambassador as a representative of the president. Thus, the ambassador made the vice-president ride on his left in the ambassador's official limousine.

Finally, we have heard a good deal of ideological rhetoric which has gradually abated in tone and been replaced by a much more moderate sort of language, as the presidential utterances in the context of the Geneva summit showed. The Reagan administration's behavior has from the beginning been quite pragmatic and restrained. The dramatic thing about their two uses of military force is that they have been so small and so limited that they point up the administration's unwillingness to use force and the recognition, on its part, of the futility of force in most situations. It is one thing to win by intervening with force as we did in Grenada. In so doing the administration underscored the fact that it was unwilling to use force in El Salvador and Nicaragua. What has been lacking, ever since Vietnam, has been a foundation for consensus that can only be rebuilt partly as a result of the passage of time, partly through the articulation of persuasive goals, and partly through performance. I think we may well be seeing, as a consequence of the lead-up to the summit—and I hope its follow-through as well—the emergence of a kind of consensus which both reflects a sense of strategy and can serve as the foundation for it.

4

A VIEW FROM THE CONGRESS

Charles McC. Mathias, Jr.

The Congress also has its perception of its interest in foreign policy. Many conflicts between the legislative and executive branches in foreign affairs derive from their different perceptions of the same circumstances, resulting from different imperatives and ideologies.

E LLIOT RICHARDSON'S REMARK that there is perception of the interests of the State Department prompts me to observe that there is a perception of interests on the part of the Congress. Many of the conflicts between the executive and the legislative branches of government in the field of foreign policy stem from the different perceptions of precisely the same circumstances. And if that is true between the White House and the State Department, it is even more true between the White House, the State Department and the Congress. Part of the perception gap appears to emanate from different imperatives and ideologies. In this country, which is now more than two centuries old and has a number of wars and crises behind it, it is still striking to find such different views and interpretations of the same problem. Whether on Vietnam or Lebanon or the Panama Canal or arms sales in the Middle East, all of us have these difficulties.

I suppose that the first question to ask is, "What does it matter?" Why is it important that the president and the majority in the Congress sometimes have different perceptions of the same circumstances? It is instructive, although very fundamental, to look at the Constitution, because the Congress at large does play a role. The power of the purse is a controlling factor in executing any national policy, so the Congress has a means of exerting its will or, at least, registering its views when the appropriations are up for votes. The ultimate act of foreign policy, the declaration of war, is not an executive act; it is a congressional act.

Beyond those general ways in which the Congress can influence these questions, however, are the very specific powers of the Senate. Under the Constitution, the Congress participates in appointing ambassadors. The Congress participates in appointing secretaries of state. It has all sorts of other, lesser acts or powers that are embodied in the Constitution, such as that exotic subject of "letters of marque" by which Congress can inflict some influence on the direction of national policy. There is also the rather extraordinary power of the Senate to ratify treaties.

This has been a feature of the American Constitution from the very beginning, and it is interesting to note that it was just recently emphasized and underscored by the Supreme Court in the famous Chadha Decision. The Chadha Decision was that decision of the court which recently cut back the powers of the Congress by declaring that a one-house veto, an action by a single house, would not constitute legislative action in ways which would nullify some of the executive intentions. However, the court specifically said in the Chadha Decision that the Senate's unreviewable power to ratify treaties negotiated by the president was one of only four provisions in the Constitution by which one house may act alone, with the unreviewable force of law not subject to the president's veto. So, here again, in a very current and contemporary expression of constitutional law, the Senate's role in foreign policy is underscored.

Of course, one of the interesting facets of American policy-making is the way in which that power is exerted by the president. It is part of our national legend that George Washington, as the first president and as the president who was creating the precedent, tried to play a part in that Senate exercise of power—the ratification of treaties—regarding an Indian treaty negotiated with one of the Indian tribes. He had his coach and four hitched up and drove down to Wall Street [he was living in New York at the time], to Federal Hall, where he got out of his yellow coach with the white horses, walked into the Senate, and announced that he was there to receive the advice and consent of the Senate on this proposed Indian treaty. One of the senators who was then president of the Senate wrote a little history of that episode. He said, "I had, at an early stage, whispered to Mr. Morris that I thought the best way to conduct the business was to have all the papers committed. My reasons were that I saw no chance of a fair investigation while the President of the United States sat there, with his Secretary of War, to support his opinions and to overawe the timid and neutral part of the Senate." Did you know there was a timid and neutral part of the Senate?

Perhaps the most distinct description of that event was one given years later by John Quincy Adams in his memoirs. He said, "Mr. Crawford told twice over the story of President Washington having at an early period of his Administration gone to the Senate with a project of a treaty to be negotiated and been present at their deliberations on it. They debated and proposed alterations, so that when Washington left the Senate, he would be damned if he went there again."

This has been a controversial power of the Senate from the very beginning, extensively considered at the Constitutional Convention, but debated in the Constitutional Convention from the point of view of ratification. Various schemes for the Constitution discussed how treaties were to be ratified; the Virginia Plan and the New Jersey Plan discussed ratification, but there were no original proposals for the negotiation of treaties. The Senate was not brought into the negotiating process, only into the ratifying process—the retrospective part of the procedure. Therein lies some part of the dichotomy of American foreign policy. The president proposes and then the Senate is expected to dispose. Of course, it was a different country in that time, and the Senate, composed of only twenty-six members, was a close and intimate body. Therefore, the difficulties that have been encountered since, the kind of controversies that have been engendered, may be built into the very process of negotiating and ratifying a treaty.

Two different views of the same acts have often, despite the increase in the speed and the amount of information available, placed the executive and legislative branches of government at odds because of difference in perspective. I must say that there is an interesting recent example in which there was more convergence than conflict in the respective views on a number of foreign policy questions, and that is the approach to the November 1985 summit meeting. Previously there was a wide divergence of views between the Congress and the Executive on how such a summit should be approached. I think that in the presummit period, the Congress and the president came together in a significant way. Without prejudging future differences, I think this is a critical consensus that strengthens the president's authority and is particularly essential in summit negotiations. Perhaps this signals a respite after a long period of contention between the executive and the legislative branches.

I would not say that we will ever speak with one voice, because that is not in our nature. However, in an increasingly complex and interdependent world in which any miscalculation can cause such tragic consequences, we may no longer have the luxury of treating some of the critical foreign policy issues as differently as night and day from one end of Pennsylvania Avenue to the other. I think that we can and we will continue to argue intensely about how we accomplish objectives abroad, but there needs to be a broader consensus on national interests. Another example of the way in which that has come about in recent days is South Africa, where there had been widely differing views at the opposite ends of Pennsylvania Avenue as to what we should do about South Africa—what our position should be towards the policy of apartheid in the Republic of South Africa. Gradually, rather painfully, and not too gracefully, we have moved, in this instance with Congress in the lead, to a position about which both parties generally agree.

Perhaps the lesson is to work a little harder to find common denominators and to become partners in conducting foreign policy, whether that involves the ultimate act of dispatching troops, voting appropriations for military or economic assistance, or the more formal process of negotiating and ratifying treaties. Our perceptions may never be identical, but they certainly should be more alike than they have been on many occasions.

There are some built-in institutional differences. These differences recur, go on from generation to generation; they are not reflective of a particular transient issue in the Congress. One such issue is that of nuclear policy. The Congress tends to be more sensitive on nuclear issues, more concerned about possible proliferation, and holds the administration's feet to the fire more closely than usual. We have had this experience not only in nuclear relations with India, but also towards Pakistan and, most recently, with respect to the People's Republic of China, where there is an impending agreement.

Therefore, one of the great challenges for any president is to set an agenda and to devise a policy that will generate congressional support for the broad policies of the country. Here is the central problem of the process; because not only have several of the recent policies been flawed, from Vietnam to Lebanon to Nicaragua, and from economic policy to energy policy, but the level of cooperation and consultation between the two branches has been erratic. In some periods, with some administrations and some committee chairmen in the Congress, there has been very good communication and consideration of the future, and discussion of alternatives and possibilities. In other periods, there has been much less communication, with confrontation more likely to result.

The Panama Canal Treaty is perhaps a classic example of both the best and the worst in the process. The treaty was ably negotiated. If there was a flaw in the negotiations, perhaps it was in the failure to consider the public presentation, the public reception of the idea. The debate in the Senate, which incidentally was the second longest debate in Senate history, rose to spectacular heights. Occasionally, however, it fell so low that it obscured some fundamental truths and the national interest as well. Senators tried in that process to become negotiators and, in the end, only narrowly averted an international crisis. Although the treaty was ratified, it had a debilitating effect on the remainder of President Carter's term.

Some opponents to the treaty predicted that the "treaty amounted to strategic annihilation." Others said that the Soviet Union and the Cubans would be running the Canal the day after the treaty was ratified. I suppose it is one of the more telling ironies of recent history that the treaty's most vocal opponent at the time benefits today from its stabilizing effect on one of the most troublesome regions of his foreign policy agenda. Perhaps that is one of the gifts that providence has cast upon the United States.

We were all well and duly warned by the great American John Hay, who spoke eighty-five years ago about the obstacles inherent in any treaty involving the Canal. Hay despaired of the Senate process of treaty ratification. He said, "I long ago made up my mind that no treaty that gave room for a difference of opinion could ever pass the Senate. But when I sat in the Canal Convention, I felt sure that no one, out of a madhouse, could fail to see the advantages on our side. I underrated the power of ignorance and spite acting upon cowardice. There will always be thirty-four percent of the Senate on the backguard of every issue. A treaty entering the Senate is like a bull going into the arena: no one can say just how or when the blow will fall, but one thing is certain, it will never leave the arena alive."

Well, John Hay's ghost might jump up and kick his heels today if he looked into the files of the Foreign Relations Committee, because there, in one form or another, lie the symbols of the difficulties of which he spoke. There are as many as forty unratified treaties that have been submitted to the Senate since the end of World War II, including the Genocide Convention and a number of economic and environmental treaties and, of course, several arms control agreements with the Soviet Union.

ı ethnic immigration to the
rly 20th centuries. What there
ndably disaffected ethnic mi-
, Finns, Ukrainians, Jews and
issionary contact—Russians
ze, but too Eastern for early
sult, the two classic ways of
d in our long era of isolation
an case. Lacking geopolitical
separated fronts in two world
r acquired any mutual under-
y of each to mirror image the
nd political, ideological, and
ween these two great mul-
tions on the periphery of Eu-
the Soviet Union in American
may be our greatest continu-
nding.

e was a centralized autocracy
vas the military and the key
ineer (the dominant profession
mmittee); whereas the United
leral democracy in which the
productive enterprise and the
meliorative lawyer (the domi-
). Ideologically, both societies
ıs with universal pretensions
ne that contains any narrowly
d States is heir to the North
tradition of a revolution for
nal republic guaranteeing indi-
f Soviet Socialist Republics is
erarchical and feudal Eastern
oeconomic equality secured in
meaning of soviet) guarantee-
hts. Psychologically, the con-
rld War II was deeply compli-
which each of these societies

I suppose that in closing the question must be asked, how can we improve the process? One of the suggestions is to change article II, section 2 of the Constitution, which requires a two-thirds majority, and make it a simple majority. However, there may be more viable alternatives. The executive is frequently tempted to evade article II, section 2 by finding other alternatives such as executive agreements, letters of understanding, and various other euphemisms for international agreements. The Case Act fairly well blocks that alternative, though, by requiring that all such agreements go to the Senate, regardless of what they are called.

There are two potentially helpful reforms that I would like to see occur in the Congress. One would be public financing of elections. Although this might seem a far-flung approach to foreign policy, if senators could be more objective and less tied to special interests in their campaigns, I believe the Senate would have more objective debates on all subjects.

The second would be radio and television coverage of Senate debates. Our single fleeting experiment, during the Panama Canal Treaty, was highly successful. We did not televise, but we did provide radio coverage of those Senate debates. This gave the American people the critical edge of understanding of that treaty. It made a difference. In fact, it made a difference to the senators personally. I used to walk around the streets during that period and people would stop me and say, "I heard you when I was in my car. I was stuck in traffic, I was listening, and I didn't know you fellows knew as much as you seem to know." I think it could make foreign policy debate come alive in this country in a way that it has not previously done.

These are obvious, but not magic, solutions. The only real solution is to follow sound policies, improve cooperation and communication between the executive and the legislative branches, and work hard to improve the process.

There was almost no Russia
United States in the 19th and ea
was came mainly from underst
norities within the empire: Pole
others. Nor was there any
were too Christian to evangeli
ecumenical familiarity. As a r
building interest in a foreign la
were both absent in the Russi
contact and fighting on totally
wars, America and Russia neve
standing. There was a tendenc
other and overlook the profo
psychological differences bet
tiethnic, continentwide civiliza
rope. Our tendency to describe
terms with American analogie
ing obstacle to serious underst

Politically, the Russian empi
in which the key institution
modernizing leader was the eng
today in the Soviet Central Co
States was a decentralized fe
key institution was the private
key modernizing leader was the
nant profession in our Congres
were legitimized by revolutio
(neither country adopting a na
ethnic designation). The Unit
Atlantic, primarily protestant
liberty secured in a constitutio
vidual civil rights. The Union
heir to the tradition born in h
Europe of a revolution for soc
communal counsels (the litera
ing social rather than civil rig
frontation of the two after Wo
cated by the different ways in

felt itself to be unique—and in some sense superior to every-one else. Russians tended to feel uniquely persecuted and conscious of their cultural inferiority to Europe, which they nonetheless brutalized as they moved their imperial border into the middle of Europe, bringing with them a peculiar anxiousness to be respected. Americans tended to feel uniquely favored and superior to a corrupt old world, which they nonetheless entered after long isolation, bringing with them a peculiar anxiousness to be loved.

The Soviet Union, of course, had discovered America in the interwar period long before America began seriously to study the Soviet Union. The United States replaced Germany during this period as the model of industry and modernity. American specialists were involved in most of the great symbolic industrialization efforts of the Stalin era (the Dne-propetrovsk Dam, the steel complex at Magnitogorsk, the tractor plant at Stalingrad, the Moscow-Khabarovsk tele-phone line); by 1940 one-third of all Soviet foreign purchases were in the United States; and with Lend-Lease aid during the wartime alliance, the American model became even more revered.

In the postwar period, however, America also replaced Germany as the personification of the hostile West—tradition-ally seen in Russia as a unitary enemy that is nonetheless morally inferior and politically divisible. We were the West that they publicly confronted even as they privately borrowed from us. We met the immediate challenges that led to the Cold War, taking over from Britain the historic task of containing the dominant power in Europe from establishing total hegem-ony over the continent or in Asia. We subsequently demon-strated to everyone free to look the inability of the stagnant communist model under Stalin's surviving protégés even to approximate, let alone "overtake" and "surpass" free econo-mies. With the long-delayed arrival of a post-Stalinist genera-tion under Gorbachev, America is now confronted with more capable leaders who have retained the military strength and global capabilities built up under Brezhnev and thus the capacity to threaten the United States in three unprecedented

ways: 1) by destroying the United States directly in minutes
or hours with nuclear missiles; 2) by reducing the United
States to vassalage in months or years by establishing geopolitical dominance in Eurasia through conventional imperial
politics; and 3) by bleeding us into subordination over the next
few decades through increasing domination in the Third
World.

Faced by an opponent with such awesome capabilities,
America clearly needed a diplomacy capable of analyzing and
probing the classic questions of the nature and intentions of
such a protagonist. But, despite a few brilliant exceptions, our
record has been rather dismal. During the fifteen years of
relative friendship that began with diplomatic recognition in
1933, politicians in America disregarded the cautionary notes
of the small cadre of professional students of Russia within
the Foreign Service and helped keep official America largely
ignorant of the monumental horror and internal genocide of
the high Stalin period. And there seemed little awareness that
diplomacy was only one wing of a dual policy the other part of
which actively worked for subversion and revolution under
the Comintern, many of whose former officials still linger on
to control contact with foreigners. Few lessons were learned
from the incredibly lengthy and unproductive negotiations of
the 1930s on minor matters. A pattern was established in the
wartime summits, which continued to the Nixon-Brezhnev
summits, of accepting general agreements at a high level,
while the Soviets make specific advances at lower levels.
This, despite endless warnings from professionals: William
Bullitt in 1936, "We should take a vow right now never to
accept anything in principle, but only to discuss concrete
detailed proposals." General John Deane in 1945, "It has
been my experience that an 'agreement in principle' means
exactly nothing to the Russians. They are therefore extremely
generous in making such agreements." I am afraid that the
already mentioned American desire to be loved played something of a role—or at least the Soviets perceived that it did—
when they attempted to overrule the inhibitions of subordi-
nate professionals by dealing directly with Roosevelt in the

late wartime period. The peculiarly American tendency to pretend that there is a commonality of interests where none exists (e.g., Roosevelt's attempts to ingratiate Stalin by criticizing Churchill) merely convinces Leninists that the Western interlocutor is manipulable and "not serious"—a mistake that would not have been made if anyone had noticed the advice that one scholar had given at the time of recognition: to deal with any Stalinist interlocutor as with a rattlesnake that will "sink its fangs impartially into hands that caress or fists that menace."

During the protracted Cold War, peace was kept—from the late forties till the early sixties through the American monopoly of strategic power and, thereafter, through the rough parity that was codified at the Nixon-Brezhnev summits of the early seventies—but has been falling apart ever since. Our small cadre of truly experienced professionals from George Kennan to Llewellyn Thompson and their generation was not really replaced, and the relatively few professionals of the next generation are often mysteriously assigned elsewhere. Détente (and its repudiation) was neither subjected to professional cross-examination nor coupled with incentives for Soviet restraint. The built-in temptations to take advantage of perceived American weakness were rendered irresistible by the compulsions in the Soviet Union to vindicate abroad an ideology that was conspicuously failing at home.

As Gorbachev, the protégé of Suslov and Andropov, moves ahead to bring the postwar, post-Stalinist generation into power, America seems still unable to craft the steady rational policy towards the Soviet Union which everyone believes we need both to avoid miscalculations on their part and to sustain unity among our allies. We are crippled by two persistent illusions about the Soviet Union. The first (or liberal) view is that liberalization is somehow built into the process of national development and can be aided by more accommodating attitudes towards Soviet leaders. This view is virtually canonical in academia, predominant in the national media, and widespread in the business community. It generally accompanies a tendency to stress underlying socioeconomic causes for world problems and America's need to adjust to other rising forces and gracefully accept a declining geopolitical role. The second (or conservative) view is that continuing Soviet hostility somehow reflects built-in historical characteristics of immutable Russian (or Bolshevik) attitudes for which there is no remedy except continuous confrontation by external force. This view is virtually canonical in the defense establishment, predominant in émigré and labor communities, and widespread throughout the country. It generally accompanies a tendency to stress communist support or instigation of world tensions and America's need to strengthen, and at times assert, its own force.

We must, in my view, reject the simplification and implied determinism of both these views. Advancing education and modernization do not lead to liberalization, as Nazi Germany showed; and while Gorbachev's better educated generation may not need to bear the guilt or perpetuate the paranoia of the Brezhnev-Chernenko generation, whose careers directly benefited from the Stalinist genocide of the 1930s, it will be a very difficult legacy to shake. The Reagan administration, by focusing on redressing the military balance, has checked the Soviet leaders' inertial inclination to believe that they could continue to register relatively cost-free gains in foreign policy. But the projecting of increased power has risked revalidating culturally to the broader Russian people precisely the historic image of a hostile West seeking material predominance that the surviving Stalinists need to justify their militaristic policies.

So the need remains for a sustainable, differentiated policy (always difficult in a democracy that wants things clear and simple)—a policy that will simultaneously 1) check the external power thrust and internal legitimization of the Stalinist oligarchs, and 2) provide rational hope and some incentive for those interested in turning to internal development and structural reform. But a crucial missing ingredient is a clear sense of what we really want from the Soviet Union—the unresolved clash between the liberal view of merely restraining their external expansion and the conservative view of working for either a breakup or a revolutionary transformation of their empire. The liberal view is more modest and certainly inherently appealing, but is in the last analysis a cop-out for dealing with a country whose external behavior results so greatly from its ideology. Great Russian imperialism never extended into the inner psyche in mental hospitals or out to Southeast Asia, southern Africa, and Central America. Responsible American leadership has the right and the obligation to try to encourage any power able to destroy us to develop structural and moral restraints against doing so. The Helsinki Final Act makes important parts of Soviet internal policy matters of international commitment; and human rights are an important part of the moral consciousness of the coming generation in the Soviet Union. The oversimplified conservative view is not the answer either, however, for it presents a Soviet leadership that has never been more Great Russian than now with what historically has been most difficult for Russians to accept: the external imposition of a foreign ideal. The more we presume to prescribe and proclaim *our* blueprint for *their* future, the more we encourage their retreat into reactionary xenophobia.

In my view, American foreign policy must focus (with the liberals) on modifying Soviet policies towards the outside world, but must understand (with the conservatives) that real changes will come only with real internal changes in the Soviet Union itself. Such changes will probably be evolutionary rather than revolutionary, and they will have to be defined by Russians for Russians—and not thought of by us as somehow representing imperfect approximations of ourselves. I have argued elsewhere for my belief that there are powerful moral and intellectual forces in Russia for the potential reconstitution of that society. However important they may prove to be, our simple, understandable foreign policy objective should be to insist that the Soviet Union directly and publicly repudiate its structural commitment to an unlimited global mission, and recognize peaceful coexistence as the basic condition of a pluralistic world rather than a temporary tactic in a continuing world revolutionary struggle. This does not

ask the impossible. Rather, it invites them to pursue unequiv-
ocally the objective of internal development that they have set
for themselves in the middle part of their current party
program—and to have the courage to pare off the unpopular
and expensive global commitments that are reasserted at the
beginning and end of the same program. Such a clear demand
goes to the source of our problem, which is not weapons or
even regional conflicts, but the global ideological commitments of the men who man the weapons and fan the conflicts.

Defining a simple, but inflexible objective could help us
sustain a steady course. An inherently moderate and nonin-
trusive demand, it should command the allegiance of our allies
and the sympathetic interest of the new generation in the
Soviet Union itself. Once we have made clear the demand we
are making on them, we will be better able to undertake—
without illusion or confusion—the two key items for which we
have a special joint responsibility: the prevention of thermo-
nuclear war and the reduction of the risks of violent confrontation at the subnuclear or regional level. However, in the
absence of a clear sense of the political-ideological nature of
the threat we face, there may be a continuation of the alarm-
ing recent trend simply to make weapons the measure of
everything else in the superpower relationship. The silent,
conservative majority may already be fixated on the thermo-
nuclear totem in a garrison state; and the anguished liberal
minority bent on eliminating or radically restructuring the
arsenal may only be adding technological carvings on the
totem pole. The only real question left may be whether our
kind of civilization will end with a bang or a whimper: burning
in space or freezing in place. Making weapons the focus of
foreign policy moves the conflict into the one area where the
Soviets have successfully competed with us (weapons pro-
duction) and away from areas where they consistently fail.

Where there is danger, there is opportunity (the famous
Chinese character reminds us); and a clear recognition of
what we oppose in the Soviet Union will free us to develop a
new agenda in those areas where there is common interest.
Perhaps we can even begin to discuss a new global agenda for

the future that will also involve other nations and be remote enough from immediate policy issues to enable them to begin climbing off their outmoded ideology without directly rejecting it. For such an uncertain, but not unhopeful future, I can foresee a diplomacy that could be far better coordinated and organized than it has been in the past for dealing with the Soviet Union and its dependencies. I would recommend four basic changes.

First of all, we need a systematic central focal point for coordinating information about, and strategy towards, the Soviet Union within the executive branch of the U.S. government. Major activities involving the Soviet Union are now conducted in at least a dozen of the principal agencies and departments of the executive branch—and I am sorry to say that there is very inadequate coordination. (We find that many often meet each other only at the weekly Wednesday functions at our Kennan Institute.) This diffusion often forces us to play a rather amateurish game of poker (waiting for the luck of the deal, relying on facial expressions) rather than the systematic game of chess that the opposition is playing.

I believe that there must be some central chess players in the U.S. government: a central mechanism for dealing comprehensively with the Soviet Union. Australia does this in dealing with Japan, and it might be that we should for Japan as well; but with the Soviet Union it seems essential. Whether in the White House or in the State Department, the nerve center of such a mechanism must be headed by someone in whom the president has full confidence, and it should include *two quite separate and distinct* top figures—both knowledgeable about the Soviet Union and Leninist systems generally: 1) someone in charge of coordinating and implementing all government policy towards the Soviet Union; and 2) someone totally divorced from policymaking to be in charge of continuous assessment of overall Soviet capabilities, strategy, and tactics.

Such a top-level leadership team is needed not only to bring our act together and reassure our allies, but also to check the quite dangerous intrusion into American policymaking in recent years of two kinds of structural deformations: 1) the tendency of political-level figures to be seduced by the aphrodisiac of elite contact with Soviet professionals (seeing dialogue as a kind of status symbol without drawing on the cumulative memory or collective expertise within the United States government), and 2) the tendency of the foreign policy bureaucracy (being forced to deal repeatedly with the Soviet professionals) subtly to accommodate themselves to Soviet procedures and thus become in some ways a kind of symbiotic extension of the Soviet system.

A second need is for a central coordinating body (also with the confidence of the president) for defining and implementing national economic policy in general—and economic policy towards the Soviet Union in particular. Economic policy must be particularly closely coordinated with our allies and with the American private sector, both of whom desperately need a single, reliable reference point in the United States government. Such a body is needed not so much to revive the illusion of manipulating the trade lever through boycotts and the like as it is, on the contrary, to reap a different kind of benefit from what is sure to be an increase in East-West trade in the years to come. Such a body could help frustrate the unfair advantage that the Soviet Union often gains by manipulating our open competitive system. Such a body could encourage business leaders not to hold back, but to carry on boldly without becoming frightened appendages of the Soviet system huddled in Moscow waiting for favors from the Ministry of Foreign Trade or from some other central control point. American (and Western) businessmen could be encouraged to insist on access to end-users, full inspection of construction sites, information on reserves, and so forth—in short, on the conditions for business they would expect elsewhere. There may be a tremendous potential for stimulating change in the Soviet Union in any genuine on-site exposure of their emerging new generation to the creative abrasions of entrepreneurial capitalism, matrix management, and so forth. There is, to be sure, a continuing serious problem of technology transfer in the military field; but our general posture (with ourselves as well as our allies) should be to open up, not hold back. The hard point will be the need to insist on genuine openness on their side—and an end to funneling American contacts through the usual Moscow manipulation centers.

A third and related need is for real reciprocity in our bilateral diplomacy. The scandal of inequality between the physical facilities and the ambassadorial access in Moscow and Washington is nothing short of a national disgrace—one that has yet to be rectified. We should have as many Americans in our embassy in Moscow as they have Russians in Washington. Give them hardship pay or leave families at home if necessary, but do not let arguments of convenience perpetuate so much Russian control of our embassy in Moscow. We should insist that the Communist Central Committee is the equivalent of our Congress (not the Supreme Soviet), since it is only in the former that decisions are made and divisions recorded. We should insist that the Soviet Union send real scholars and not nomenklatura officials on academic exchanges; and move towards regional, professional, and even purely randomized exchanges to ensure that visits to America are part of a broadening dialogue and not merely a form of political patronage for party officials. It is important to repeat and sustain such demands in order to encourage those inside the system who may be arguing for more openness and a change of policy but who cannot make the argument themselves.

Finally, and perhaps most important, a word about the role of diplomacy in the technical "embassy" sense. I am inclined to be skeptical even about the need for embassies in many parts of the world with the advances in communication and massive direct links that we have with many countries. But embassies are very important in communist countries. They have unique abilities to establish contacts with people and places, assess intangibles, and make symbolic acts that can rapidly become part of the folklore of the oral counterculture in closed societies. We need deep study of this problem that is not simply self-justificatory and anecdotal.

We must develop in dealing with the Soviet Union and other

closed communist societies a broader spectrum of policy instruments, so that a rich civil society with a strong private sector can help open up a closed state system with a monopoly of power and a tendency to funnel all Western contact through a few central control points. In addition to a more aggressive economic policy involving the private sector and the expanded cultural and educational exchanges, I am a great believer in congressional exchanges and in counterpart exchanges with sister cities, comparable republics with states, and so forth. If we insist on reciprocity, it might be possible to have different people involved on their side and to break the incredible hammerlock that a very few apparatchiks in Moscow institutes still hold over almost all contact with Americans in ostensibly "private" bilateral meetings.

I particularly believe in the value of having American elected officials at all levels involved in dialogue with the Soviet Union. American elected officials tend to ask tougher and blunter questions than most professional diplomats—and to explain America with special authority. Whether or not our embassy in Moscow can find ways of breaking a little more out of its ghetto existence is hard for an outsider to determine; but the embassy can, at the very least, make itself a nerve center and coordinating reporter, if not something like a quarterback for the many Americans who do go to the Soviet Union and have a wider variety of access and travel possibilities.

The diplomats of the future dealing with communist systems will need high linguistic competence, experience in, and a certain zest for, ideological discussion and political conflict, and a clear sense of American values and the grass roots point of view in their own country. To be thought truly "serious" by the Soviets, our future diplomats could perhaps use occasional immersion in grass roots American attitudes. The somewhat closed, Washington-oriented world of the Foreign Service is not always clearly linked to basic American values, which, after all, differ somewhat from the dominant values of the elite media and research universities—the world of discourse in which American diplomats tend to feel most comfortable.

Diplomacy as it was perfected in the 270 years between the Treaty of Westphalia and the Versailles Conference (between the religious wars of the 17th century and the ideological conflicts of the 20th) is not really fully applicable for dealing with a monolithic Leninist state in the age of total war and totalitarian peace. Real negotiations on the important questions separating us, particularly highly technical ones like arms control, will almost certainly continue to be conducted at the high political level. And while embassies should be kept better informed about these matters than in the past, the function of embassies in communist countries will probably remain that of facilitators of dialogue conducted largely by others and a base camp for seeking out information and attitudes in the host country. If there were more centralized mechanisms in Washington for determining policy towards the Soviet Union, embassies might be given more leeway for negotiation and exploration on the spot in the future. But even if embassies will be able to perform only a rather modest role as in the recent past, special training beyond language and area expertise will be needed. A cadre of professionals devoted to this special kind of diplomacy could give greater continuity and stability to our dealings with the communist world. Regimes such as Vietnam, Cuba, and Ethiopia will require a new type of American representation, when the time comes for more normal relations with these countries. We will need tough, inwardly secure people, specially trained to deal with professional Leninists and not under the impression that they are dealing with just another Third World country. Only those who combine toughness with expertise will ultimately be trusted by the American people to attest that real change has come, if it does, and to cut a deal that is genuinely solid.

If the West can remain tough and united without being provocative in the difficult period ahead, and can undertake new initiatives without reviving old illusions, there may be reasons for cautious hope that the Soviet Union may ultimately move beyond the nationalism of the military-police establishment (the current fallback position from a decaying communist faith for the ruling oligarchy) and develop some new identity by the twenty-first century that is presently unforeseen by either them or us. This could be a constructive evolution that draws on both old Russian tradition and recent outside experience rather than on the destructive revolutionary ideology and the dangerous international politics of recent Soviet history. Let us hope that we will have the intelligence and imagination to analyze and understand this process and the organization and discipline to help promote it.

6

DIPLOMACY IN OPEN SOCIETIES

Berndt von Staden

Transnational cooperation has in recent years grown so much in scope and intensity that the distinction between which matters are predominantly domestic and which foreign has become less sharp.

T O THIS DAY our conception of diplomacy is to a large degree influenced by the era of the classical "cabinet-policy" of Europe in the seventeenth, eighteenth, and nineteenth centuries. We still use this model as a yardstick for evaluating the conditions under which modern diplomacy operates.

The beginning of the relatively short era of classical European diplomacy coincides with the end of the religious wars and with the emergence of Richelieu as the foremost European statesman. Its heyday brings to mind the names of Kaunitz, Talleyrand, and Metternich. Classical diplomacy began its decline with the emergence of nationalism in the nineteenth century, and ended with the disintegration of Bismarck's European system.

With the notable exceptions of Britain, Venice, and later the United States, the following was characteristic of classical diplomacy: the determination of foreign policy was the prerogative of the monarch, who was considered to be the sole source of authority in the field of external relations. He was assisted by a small number of personal advisors, his cabinet secretaries, hence the name "cabinet-policy."

The execution of the monarch's foreign policy decisions, or in other words, the conduct of diplomacy, was almost exclusively entrusted to members of one single class—the aristocracy. They were not professionals in the modern sense of the word but, by serving for many years, they were what today we would call career officials. They formed a rather homogeneous, cosmopolitan, and internationally interrelated class, and considered themselves to be born servants of the Crown in the service of the armed forces and of diplomacy. They owed greater allegiance to the person of the monarch than to a country. In continental Europe, to go from the service of one sovereign to another was neither infrequent nor objectionable.

With the exception of Britain and the United States, foreign policy and the conduct of diplomacy were neither checked nor even influenced by elected representatives of the people, public opinion, or the media. America did not play a central role in those days, and in Britain only a limited number of people, mostly aristocrats, had any influence on the making and conduct of foreign policy.

Domestic considerations, therefore, had little impact on shaping external relations. Secrecy was considered one of the basic rules of the decision-making process on the political level as well as in conducting diplomacy. The social, structural, and political differences between the states which formed the "Concert of Powers" were considerable, but ideological as well as religious factors did not, as a rule, greatly influence their relations. The parties to the "Concert" were therefore interchangeable. They were able to form changing alliances which facilitated maintaining a balance of power.

International relations were largely limited to "power politics," and sometimes even to the "family politics" of the reigning dynasties and to a certain amount of trade. Interdependence in the modern sense was unknown.

War was considered an acceptable and legitimate instrument of foreign policy, or as Clausewitz put it, a continuation of policy by other means. War in those times was limited in nature and remained as a rule under political control. Despite recurrent wars, the system was thus relatively stable. Occasional changes of alliance notwithstanding, the policy of the major powers was characterized by a relatively high degree of continuity and predictability.

The foregoing overview is necessarily short and simple, but shows clearly how extensively the conditions under which diplomacy operates have changed since then. This is more particularly true for the West than for authoritarian or totalitarian regimes in socialist countries of the East or the Third World.

The monarch as the source of a more or less undivided authority in foreign affairs has disappeared. Foreign policy is now largely the prerogative of the executive branch of government. In practice, as in the case of the United States, it also comes under the concurrent authority of the legislative branch. The political parties increasingly play a background role. Furthermore, in open societies, making foreign policy and conducting diplomacy are public affairs, increasingly dependent on public opinion, and hence on the media as well.

There are several reasons for this development, five of which are particularly significant.

First: International cooperation in modern times is growing in scope and intensity, particularly among industrialized democracies, as well as in developing countries. It covers a broader spectrum of activities in the political, economic, financial, monetary, technological, and scientific fields. This growing interdependence increasingly makes external relations in western societies a matter of domestic concern. The distinction between issues that are predominantly domestic or predominantly foreign, such as monetary policy or national security policy, is less sharp than in the past. This trend continues.

Second: This blurring of the line is further reinforced by the ever-increasing role which the media play in open societies. Their opinion-forming influence can hardly be overestimated. As a consequence, next to nothing is left of the traditional rule of secrecy in formulating foreign policy and in conducting diplomacy. Foreign policy decisions are being publicly discussed and made, and are subject to various domestic influences and pressures. Nothing like a "pure" foreign policy exists any longer.

Third: The factors just mentioned can easily lead to a certain lack of consistency in foreign policy. Furthermore, they expose the conduct of diplomacy to the constant pressures of impatience and myopic historical memory, characteristic of an open society. Recurrent changes brought about by elections tend to increase the lack of continuity and predictability in the foreign policy of modern democracies.

Fourth: Ideology and morality play a growing role. This applies primarily, but not exclusively, to East-West relations. Ideological and emotional factors influence foreign relations elsewhere also; for example, with respect to rightist or racist regimes and cases of human rights violations.

And finally, fifth: The professionals have lost ground, as the tasks of shaping foreign policy and conducting diplomacy have become highly complex and diversified and can no longer be the exclusive domain of a closed group of professional diplomats. They are even virtually excluded from some undertakings. This is particularly true concerning financial and monetary affairs, as well as scientific and technological endeavors, but it also applies to economic relations.

The influence of professional diplomats is being increasingly reduced, but not simply for reasons of competence. Political developments, as well as progress in the fields of communication and transportation, also play a role. Today, heads of state and government, as well as cabinet members and others in authority, are able to communicate directly with each other without using diplomats as intermediaries. At the same time, party interests and considerations of loyalty exercise a growing influence on personnel decisions. Almost everywhere in the Western world, the involvement of political appointees in formulating and executing foreign policy is growing, and the involvement of professional diplomats is decreasing. The career diplomat is even losing ground in the more traditional field of political relations.

In trying to assess these developments, one should first of all apply one of the classical rules of diplomacy—to take the world as it is. It does not make any sense to complain about things that are inevitable or to obstinately oppose historic trends. The times of Metternich and of his secret diplomacy are gone, a fact which even Henry Kissinger, the outstanding diplomat of our time, has come to accept. One also has to accept that contemporary foreign policy is made and carried out in the "open," that media pressure and public opinion exercise the strongest influence, and that legislatures, with their changing majorities, demand their share in the decision-making process, not only with respect to the formulations of foreign policy guidelines, but increasingly in operational matters. To some extent at least, one must also accept the reduced role professional diplomats play in international relations.

Some conclusions can be drawn from all this. In view of the various pressures and constraints mentioned, it is obviously no easy task in an open society to conceive a carefully considered foreign policy, to keep it on a steady course, and to carry it out effectively.

However, this is only the more negative side of the coin. Open societies may be unwieldy but, mainly as a result of freely expressed public opinion, they are also inclined to be cooperative and peace loving. As can be demonstrated, the Helsinki Final Act is basically correct in stating that "respect for human rights is an essential factor for peace, justice and well-being necessary to ensure the development of friendly relations and cooperation among . . . all states."

In the relations of democracies with each other, foreign policy and diplomacy in the classical sense are increasingly losing importance. War between countries of the Western world, or between industrialized democracies, has become quite unthinkable. Traditional barriers in the economic, financial, and monetary fields are increasingly being removed, and policies in those fields are viewed and handled as matters of common concern. Agencies of Western governments communicate and cooperate directly with each other. In short, relations between open societies are beginning to acquire a new character. They no longer fall into the category of foreign relations in the traditional sense, and they do not yet belong to the realm of domestic policy. However, they are coming increasingly close to it, as demonstrated by the example of the European Community and of the industrialized democracies associated with it.

In the context of the present analysis, the essential point here is that open societies, as experience shows, have no particular problems in coping with the conditions under which their mutual relations are to be handled. They can live quite well with each other, and to that extent the future of diplomacy in the West does not seem to pose particularly serious problems.

The real problems for contemporary and future Western diplomacy lie elsewhere, in the relationship of open societies with nondemocratic societies, in particular with communist or, as they call themselves, socialist regimes. As indicated earlier, democracies by their very nature tend to have nonantagonistic relations with each other. In contrast, the relationship of socialist with nonsocialist societies has, according to the teachings of Marxism-Leninism, by necessity an antagonistic character. It can at best be only partially cooperative. It is essentially competitive, not so much in the Western sense of commercial competition, but more in the sense of a zero-sum contest. Within the framework of this kind of antagonistic relationship, the conduct of Western diplomacy is, of course, greatly affected by the various constraints and pressures to which it is subjected.

This is all the more true because the decision-making process, as well as the conduct of diplomacy in closed and, particularly, in socialist countries, is subject to entirely different conditions. True, such differences are not all disadvantageous to open societies. For instance, socialist societies operate under the handicaps of ideological narrow-mindedness and rigidity, of insurmountable mistrust, and often of paralyzing overcentralization. However, they have an advantage in other respects. In the execution of foreign policy, they come much closer to the classical model than does the diplomacy of Western-style democracies. The influence of domestic interests on their foreign policy is limited. The same is true of public opinion, although it is not altogether insignificant. There is a strong element of continuity in foreign policy under one-party rule. The conduct of diplomacy is almost exclusively entrusted to well-trained and experienced professionals. Last but not least, in socialist societies both the decision-making process and the conduct of diplomacy are still wrapped in secrecy.

As indicated, the parallels between East and West discussed here are partially disadvantageous to the latter. The question is whether anything can be done about it.

The basic conditions under which open societies function cannot be changed. It would be not only senseless but also self-defeating to attempt such changes, because pluralism and openness in the broadest sense are precisely what the West stands for and what it could not disavow without abandoning its precepts. What might on first view look like weakness, however, could possibly be turned to advantage. As humankind enters the age of communication, this is probably true with respect to pluralism and openness, as opposed to any ultimately vain attempt to seal off one's own society and to preserve its monolithic structure. In that respect, the West is obviously in consonance with the mainstream of history.

In the age of information, public discussion and formulation of foreign policy can and should be turned into a powerful tool for the conduct of external relations. There is no other way to build and maintain the national consensus, the only precept in an open society on which a carefully considered, firm, and steady foreign policy can be based. There is also probably no other way in which to further the evolution of a more open society in the East.

Regarding the execution of foreign policy and the conduct of diplomacy, things look quite different. In these matters, Western diplomacy continues to require a high degree of discipline and professionalism for handling antagonistic relationships, particularly with the Eastern countries, and this does not contradict what has been said earlier. Any country that wants to stand firm, no matter how open its society might be, can have only one foreign policy. Therefore, foreign policy decisions, once made, must be executed faithfully and efficiently and must not be attacked by leaks and other questionable means. This rule is not at all at variance with the principles on which an open society is based. As an institution, the government needs loyal and competent servants, as does any institution, whether private or public. In a way, governments need them even more, because more is at stake. An open society also needs secrecy in executing—though not in formulating—its foreign policy, particularly when matters of national security are involved.

This is where professionalism has a role to play. As already indicated, foreign relations in our day are much more complex and multilayered than they were in the classical era of diplomacy. Furthermore, the risks involved are much greater if the relationship under consideration is of an antagonistic nature. War has not only become unthinkable between democracies; even among opponents it is no longer considered a legitimate means of policy. Everyone agrees that war between the major powers would be the ultimate disaster. Although this seems to be a change for the better, it is not due to a change in human nature. It is simply a reflection of the incredibly dangerous nature of modern weapons. They are much too dangerous to be used for any political purpose.

Meanwhile, mistrust continues to result in an arms race, and the arms race in turn generates additional mistrust. Nobody has a way of knowing for certain where all this will lead. We all have every reason to ardently wish the president of the United States good luck and full success in his endeavor to improve the chances for lasting peace.

It is vitally important for every political leader to have at his side aides and advisors of the highest professional caliber, whether we call them diplomats or something else. What is important is that they understand what they are doing and that they know how to go about it. One can learn all this, of course, just as banking or business management can be learned. The point is, it must be learned. Good bankers do not fall from heaven, nor do good managers of foreign relations. In these dangerous times, we entrust to the latter much more than the conduct of foreign affairs.

7

A EUROPEAN LOOKS AT DIPLOMACY

Emanuel de Margerie

The Common Market, the Council of Europe, and other European forums have changed and invigorated the old diplomacy. This should lead to a subordination of national susceptibilities in implementing the letter of the European treaties, which will often require within the Community a resort to majority voting.

I WILL BEGIN with a personal anecdote to show how the environment of diplomacy can change. Some eighty years ago, at the turn of the century, my grandfather was Counsellor at the French Embassy here in Washington at a time the city had only fourteen diplomatic missions. One used to go out riding with the president's daughter. America had not yet taken on the world role it has since assumed; and I would venture to say that the concept of the Western world was something that probably existed subconsciously, but I do not think that anyone was using the term as a matter of everyday conversation.

Eighty years later, there are one hundred forty diplomatic missions in this city, and America has become a major power in the world and assumed worldwide responsibilities. I think that the concept of the Western world is one with which we constantly live, whether or not we define it. Now, I have asked myself two questions. One is, what is the Western world? I will try to go into a few details on that question.

What is the Western world, I asked myself? I was disconcerted because I could find no clear definition. I wondered whether there really was a Western world. Of course, there is a Western world, but it is never the same. It is not an object of strict definition. You will perhaps be astonished to hear this coming from a Frenchman, but I do not think that we need be too Cartesian about it.

It seems to me that the Western world is something which oscillates somewhere between the Atlantic Alliance and the Free World. It is obviously broader than the Atlantic Alliance. It is obviously not as broad as the whole Free World. It is somewhere in between. It is a concept that incorporates elements of security; in other words, we do have a binding, common security interest in the defense of the values in which we believe. It is also a world in which we have common preoccupations in the economic field—a world where there are certain traditions and customs that are accepted by the community as a whole. I think that the Western world could perhaps be defined by the Organization for Economic Cooperation and Development. As you see, there are three very different groups: the Atlantic Alliance, the OECD, and the Free World as a whole, but there is a common link. We do have similar institutions; we have economic patterns that can be very different from one country to another but which do allow for a measure of private initiative; and we all feel that there is something in common between us.

I will tell you why I said that I think it is unwise to want to be too precise. It is not in the interest of the Western world, I think, to define its boundaries too sharply. We are related, all of us, to other parts of the world, and if you get a feeling of very strict boundaries, you are bound to have a feeling of difference between yourself and the others. I think the essence of diplomacy is so often to try to find common points of view. If we had the feeling that something stiffens the separation between us and the Mediterranean world, for instance, we would be very much the poorer for it. If one has the feeling that the Mediterranean world is in some way linked to the Western world, then what is the Mediterranean world? Is it not, for instance, the countries of Western Europe and the countries of North Africa? There again we have bonds that must be allowed to permeate the relationship with the countries of North Africa which belong to Islam. Therefore, the Western world must have a relationship with Islam.

Now, you have got the same problem with Central and Latin America. In other words, I do not think it is in our interest to separate ourselves too much from the Third World. I also think we must remain conscious that where we have something in common, we must not adopt what I would call Soviet bloc policies. We must not act as a bloc, because it hardens reality and it does not allow us to take the full measure of what we can be doing in a free and affluent society.

And now, my second point. There is one element in the Western world which strikes me and which I think will not be challenged, and that essentially concerns the relationship between America and European countries. The European component of the Western world is of great importance to the United States.

Here I may perhaps digress with a personal observation. Before becoming ambassador in Washington, I was ambassador in London; and I have noticed that Europe seen from a European point of view is not the same as the Europe seen from this country. When I look at the press, for instance, I constantly see European countries mentioned as nations and, indeed, we are nation-states. None of us think that we have renounced our national tradition. But when we see ourselves in Europe and from a European point of view, we think of ourselves differently. We think of ourselves as Europeans and as an emerging European entity which is developing through institutions of its own. There is a European rapport with the Western world—not only with the outside world, but within itself. That European world, the other essential component of the West apart from this great country, is a world which is in the making. Therefore, there is an element of ambiguity and frequently of hesitation.

I would submit that this hesitation and the quarrels which have sometimes accompanied what we call the construction of Europe must not blind one to the reality of what we have been doing among ourselves. The European Community is, of course, the essential European institution. It is not the only one. Europe would be very much the poorer if we did not establish a close relationship with other European countries belonging to the Western world that are not members of the Community. These countries are all gathered into the Council of Europe.

It is a fact, however, that in the last twenty years, the main stimulus has come from the existence of a Community which was willed as an institution. You know that the pattern of the development of American life, the gathering of a number of states into a great union, certainly had its strong influence on the founding fathers of the Community. The results obtained have not yet been equivalent to what was hoped for, and very often I think that there is a spirit of pessimism, a spirit which is often defined by the name of Europessimism. I would strongly plead with you not to let yourselves be influenced by the fashionable concept of Europessimism. It is an easy concept. I do not think it always fits the realities of the situation. After all, if you look at the development of your own constitutional procedures and existence, we Europeans, as I once heard Mr. Raymond Barre say, are not doing too badly: we are at the point where you were in 1804. "Where were you in 1804, where are you now?" Therefore, please give us a little time.

This is not to say that we have not already done a great deal, however. We have established both a common trade policy and a common agricultural policy. I would like to refer to what Ambassador von Staden says in chapter 6. He makes what I think is a very essential point; it is that the difference between what in the old language of diplomacy was called foreign policy and internal politics has now been completely blurred. For us, essential elements of our life in all the countries of Western Europe gathered together in the European Economic Community are decided in Brussels, within our Community. They are no longer the decisions of a national government. We have abdicated our national independence in a number of fields. The French do not consider themselves the only ones who are entitled to shape the future of French agriculture. Our partners are also entitled to their opinions.

What is the consequence of this? It is that there is now a totally new form of diplomacy. There are European diplomacy meetings, committees, groups of experts coming from the different ministries, arbitration between the different ministries in every national capital, and delegations coming from these national capitals to the Community capital in Brussels. The procedures are completely different. The odd thing about it is that, at a moment when the art of negotiation has partly deserted diplomatic life, negotiation has come back to us in other forms. We negotiate in European forums. There is not only observation and reporting, there are opposing points of view. Whether this is always as fruitful as it ought to be is a matter of judgment. I personally think that the national sensitivities to which we have had to cater have sometimes been too strong. It would be wise to examine whether we could, in the future, fully implement the letter of the treaties which have bound us together, and see whether we could more often resort to majority voting within the Community. This is essential if we are to keep our momentum alive.

One other point: Our problem is not only trying to find a common purpose, but also finding a common purpose with our allies in the Western world. I would like to give you an example. We are now experiencing complicated commercial problems between the European Community and the United States. The essential part of the story is the common relationship which we have now established. There is a diplomatic mission of the Community in this country, and the other day, we, the ambassadors of the Community, were called in by the U.S. Trade Representative. But whom did he call in with us? He called in the representative of the European Communities, Sir Roy Denman, who represents European interests. This is important because this administration had made certain decisions. You know that, in the field of trade, feelings sometimes do run rather high. Decisions are made; counterdecisions, reprisals, counterreprisals take place; and it so happened that a decision had been made which was hurting one of our

partners, our Italian partner. Special duties were being levied
on pasta coming from Italy. It is possible that, in the usual
circumstances of life, Italy would have a hard time defending
its pasta interests before the current administration. However, when the common diplomatic representative of ten [now
twelve] European Community members comes and says,
"This is our common position, and we do not accept what has
been done to Italian pasta and, if you persist, we will be
obliged ourselves to take countermeasures," then obviously it
has more weight.

What does all this mean? It just means that we are now
moving towards a state of affairs in the Western world where
the United States and its partners are beginning to feel an
emerging relationship of greater equality. I will not attempt to
measure the rapport between the two. It is so obvious that the
United States has power which is commensurate with its
responsibility in the world, and we fully acknowledge this.
However, I think it makes for a much healthier Western world
if there can be something more equal in our relations—if there
can be more normal give and take in the relationship between
the countries which constitute the Western world.

I would think that this applies not only to the economic
sphere but also to the field of defense and security. And there,
as Europeans, we do have a problem I would like to mention.
We are members of the Atlantic Alliance. The Atlantic Alliance is something absolutely vital and essential. We cannot
conceive of our security not being within the sphere of the
Atlantic Alliance; but at the same time we think that if we
want to contribute as a valid global partner in the Alliance, it
would be good for us to voice common European viewpoints
which may differ from those of the United States. This is a
delicate subject. It is not easy to combine the general framework, which is paramount—the Alliance—with something
which gives a European flavor to our common will-power in
European countries to bring our individual, national, corporate European contribution to the healthy functioning of the
Alliance. But this is something we want to do, and I would
think that it is in the interest of your country. Indeed, the

United States recognized a number of years ago, in the NATO/Ottawa Declaration, that some of the elements of the European scene, particularly the two nuclear forces of Great Britain and France, could be useful in the global deterrence of the Western world vis-à-vis the Soviet Union and the Soviet bloc. As a consequence, the European contribution is accepted as an important element of a global world equilibrium.

I have spoken as a Frenchman, as a European, as a member of the Atlantic community, but it seems to me that we can still see wider horizons for the Western world. We are now moving towards something which is a new concept—a concept of a world order, a world economic order being perhaps the first installment.

When I was here fifteen years ago, as deputy chief of mission at the French Embassy, I think one would have defined the Western world as something that combined the United States and Canada with the European group of nations. Now another important element has come in. Japan is becoming a member of the Western world, perhaps not so much in the field of security as in the field of a very important, developing economic relationship—a fact that raises problems.

The acceptance of Japan as part of the Western world has led to a broader definition of the Western world, as exemplified by the summit meetings of industrial nations. There were the traditional Western nations—the United States and Canada, Great Britain, Germany and France—and now a new nation, Japan, is considered part of the Western world. The first intimation of a world order might well be in these new meetings of our chiefs of state and government, trying to work out a system that falls between the old Western world and a new Western world oriented towards a world economic system.

8

A THIRD
WORLD VIEW

K. Shankar Bajpai

In international diplomacy there is no Third World, only the powerful nations and those less powerful. The less powerful countries suffer in their decision making and diplomacy through lack of the accurate and full information available to those more powerful.

I SHALL ATTEMPT to present the viewpoints, approaches, and inputs of what is called the Third World. I believe that probably the best contribution I could make is to find a better categorisation. I dislike the phrase, with its almost androgynous connotations, but I am afraid I have not been able to come up with anything better. No one word seems to suffice. We have in the past spoken of underdeveloped, or developing, or nonaligned countries. These words suggest one or another aspect of that particular group of countries we have in mind, but there is a larger concept involved which these words do not bring out. I raise this question of definition because it provides a useful point of departure for considering both the problems the Third World countries themselves face and those that they raise in the general international environment in which all countries have to function.

I hate alliteration, but the characteristics of this group of countries relevant to our examination of the future of diplomacy happen to begin with the same letter: They are all countries that have been dominated in one way or another, they are and feel disadvantaged and disregarded, and their international activity is conditioned by the desire to overcome their traditional handicaps. They almost think of themselves as countries of the world to come. In sum, they are countries that feel they have never had an effective (as distinct from purely vocal) say in international affairs to the extent they should. They believe that the development of a new international system, a new framework of international diplomacy, can give their countries—representing two-thirds of humankind—a greater voice and greater influence.

Perhaps, to explain what I mean, I should first also venture another definition of what exactly we are talking about when we say diplomacy. It must be clearly distinguished from foreign policy, with which it is too often confused. In many ways diplomacy bears to foreign policy the relationship that tactics bears to strategy. The latter determines the objectives, the former the means to achieve them. Ambassador McGhee has said that in its broadest sense diplomacy covers "all negotiations . . . intended to lessen tension or bring about agreements." However, in the essential overall framework of what each country has to do with other countries, diplomacy amounts to neither more nor less than trying to influence the decision-making process in those other countries.

This is an enormously complicated endeavour, especially as the decision-making process in each country has become more complex and as the instruments available to some countries for influencing the decision-making process in Third World countries has increased. Needless to say, every country, irrespective of the particular world to which it belongs, has two primary foreign policy objectives: to preserve national security and to promote economic well-being. Those are the ultimate objectives which must be served by diplomacy, and frankly speaking, a Third World country is no different in this respect from any other except that it is new to the game and does not yet have the instruments available to the older established countries.

We all must deal with new problems, and I agree that there is a need to update and, in fact, bring back into full play the professionalism, expertise, and good sense that we traditionally have associated with diplomacy. As Bacon used to say, we must "constantly find new remedies as time breedeth new mischiefs." God knows, there is enough mischief around us to require new remedies. Any new methodologies that can be developed will be welcomed by all, especially by those of us who are new to the game. What worries us—and I hope you will bear with me if I seem a little out of tune with the prevailing ethos—what seems to us most unfortunate is that the game remains the same as always.

There is a widespread view that there used to be a halcyon time when good, quiet, professional diplomats set about keeping the world in order by good, quiet, diplomatic methods, and that the intrusion of too many countries, of too many means of communication, of too many foreign ministers flying around all over the place, has somehow made it more difficult to deal with. Undoubtedly, the older forms of diplomacy did achieve many successes, but, good God, didn't they make an awful mess of it also? How many, many crises they created, how blind they were, and how ham-handed! One could go through history and find many successes achieved by the old diplomacy, but ultimately it was also responsible for the two greatest wars in history. One must look at the faults of the old diplomacy, as well as try to find a revival of the professionalism which, I am sure everyone agrees, up to a point at least, is essential to the conduct of international relations. Methodology apart, when it comes to the basic facts of international life, it seems to us that things have not changed very much at all.

I had sworn to myself that I would not bring up Harold Nicolson, but one can hardly talk of diplomacy without falling back on him sooner or later. I would like to draw to your attention a key point that he brought out and that still continues to bother us. Discussing the change from the old diplomacy to the new, he maintained that in former times Europe was regarded as the most important of all the continents. Asia and Africa were viewed as areas for imperial, commercial, or missionary expansion; Japan, when she arose, appeared an exceptional phenomenon; America remained isolated behind her oceans and her doctrine. No war could become a major war unless one of the five major European powers became involved. It was thus in the chancelleries of Europe alone that the final issue of general peace or war would be decided.

It was assumed that the Great Powers were greater than the small powers, since they possessed a more extended range of interests, wider responsibilities and, above all, more money and more guns. The small powers were rated in order of importance according to their military resources, their strategic position, their value as markets or sources of raw material, and their relations to the balance of power. There was nothing stable about such categories. At any one moment, one country or another would acquire prominence as a point of Anglo-French, Anglo-Russian, or Slav-Teuton rivalry or become a focus of diplomatic concern. Throughout this period, the small powers were assessed according to their effect upon the relations between the Great Powers. There was seldom any idea that their interests and opinions, much less their votes, could thwart a policy agreed upon by the "Concert of Europe."

Give or take a few countries, and the names may vary, are we not still, on the whole, facing exactly the same situation of a handful of major powers determining the course of events in the world? It seems to us, who have not had the experience or the involvement in international affairs of the older states, that we are, after an effort to get away from that world, moving back into it. I do not wish to appear naive, nor am I trying to make a virtue out of our weakness, but perhaps the approach that the entire world embarked upon when the Third World started to become independent needs to be viewed afresh and with greater sympathy.

It is not fashionable nowadays to talk of conducting international relations through international organisations, though that was in vogue when we appeared on the world scene. Then, for the first time, we became international actors in our own right, whereas before we had been in the interplay of the great power forces. We thought that a new institutional framework of multilateral diplomacy, and especially of multilateral institutions, would afford a new system for keeping peace and lessening tensions and for bringing about the additional types of understanding and agreements that Ambassador McGhee refers to as the purposes of diplomacy. I am afraid that that whole approach is in disarray and, what is worse, in disrepute. Therefore, those of us who come from the so-called Third World are finding it increasingly difficult to see how we should set about achieving our objectives.

Those objectives are basically the same as anyone else's, though we may have particular priorities. Let us take as an example of the latter the Third World's emphasis on a North-South dialogue for bringing about a climate of opinion in which the transfer of resources to developing countries can be made on easier terms than the developed world now likes to consider worthwhile. How do we set about it? Being deficient in the instrumentalities for influencing decision making in other countries, ultimately we can only hope that the other countries concerned will see that it is to their advantage to have the kind of cooperation and understanding we thought were developing in the immediate postwar world. We realize that our own efforts to contribute to this framework have not always been as conscientious as the world would like them to be.

We recognize that we have had our problems with each other, and perhaps have even created problems with the larger international community; but by and large, we have tried to build up that respect for an international community which the older powers seem to be moving away from. Therefore, for us, the challenge of the new diplomacy for the next twenty years is not only to devise new methodologies, but also to bring back a certain consciousness of the significance of giving Third World countries a voice that helps them, in turn, give their people a sense of confidence in the future. Without that, I am afraid we will return to the world of power politics and to the world of the international balance of power. I suppose that has been the historic fact of life and, to some extent, will always remain so. But we must keep trying to see whether we can avoid reverting to that purely bilateral form of diplomacy which, whatever its successes, has also suffered many failures.

In brief, the Third World countries have the same key objectives as those of the other two worlds and have to follow the same methodologies of diplomatic effort, but they are handicapped in two respects. They must function in an international environment still largely determined by the other two worlds, and they do not have the instruments available to the older established countries. As an example of the latter, one of the most important is the dissemination of information on which decisions are based. I do not wish to go over the controversy about what Third World countries have been seeking as a new information order. It is a particularly touchy subject in this country. But surely it will be agreed that most countries in the world still have to depend on what the major countries put out. The virtual creation of information on which we have to base ourselves is in limited hands that can thus create a climate in which real facts have less influence than what is disseminated by these limited circles.

Of course, Third World countries have their own strengths, especially now the capacity to resist pressures and, I must also acknowledge, the capacity to create problems. Their great hope, however, was to be able to contribute to the international scene through that currently undervalued system of multilateral institutions whose development coincided with their own emergence after World War II. Instead, today there is the tendency already cited of reverting to power politics, to the balance of power—essentially, decisions by a few powers, whatever you may prefer to call it. The Third World is thus confronted with the dual problem of how to cope with this tendency and of how to cope with the other changes that everyone faces—through telecommunications, aeroplanes, media, summitry, and so forth.

For our diplomacy, these all lead to two complexities. Decision making *within* a country involves an increasing number of influences and inputs. Decision making in *other* countries is subject to an increasing number of instrumentalities for influence. In each country, the decision-making process has become immensely complex. The number of factors that go into the process in the United States is almost incomprehensible to people who have come from countries that do not have to face such situations. In this country, for instance—and I would like to avoid giving this an order of precedence, but just to enumerate—you have Congress, the media, the business world, the academic world, the cultural world, and the ethnic groups. Not least, there is the administration itself and the whole labyrinthian government with which we have to contend. We have to try to keep up with as many of these elements as possible. This is less true of our relations with many other countries, which are purely or largely government-to-government. Here it is exciting, but also enormously difficult. You cannot escape the complexity.

I would like to agree with Ambassador McGhee that we should try to leave it more to the professionals, but this will not happen. All of us have to adjust to new methods. As an example, I was addressing Southeast Asian scholars in Madison, Wisconsin one day, bankers in New York the next, and the following evening was privileged to open the great Boston exhibition of Indian art. These are the ways we have to function. We have to reach out to these various groups in the United States, as we have to do in other countries to a greater or lesser degree, but ultimately how does it affect them?

Those of us from Third World countries can all try to have an impact on your decision making by talking to these various groups, but with very few exceptions, none of us can hope to match what you do elsewhere, much less what the real decision makers here can do to neutralise our efforts.

It has been said of Metternich that the "champion of stability went to the grave without realising that change is the law of life, that the French Revolution had a constructive as well as destructive side, that the status quo which satisfied the aristocracy was not good enough for the third and fourth estates; that the common man would grow up if he had his chance never crossed his mind." In many ways, the Third

World countries feel they are in the position of the third or fourth estates in this quotation from S.P. Gooch, and many in the other two worlds are very much like Metternich.

To sum up, I frankly see one simple conclusion: Although I keep using this phrase, there is really no such thing as the Third World when it comes to international diplomacy. I basically feel that we are dealing with the international version of Disraeli's two nations, the rich and the poor. Similarly, there are just two worlds: one of the powerful, and one of the weak or less powerful. Most of us in the Third World belong to the latter category. We have to work with all of you from the very powerful countries to try to achieve our objectives. The methodologies we have to adopt are those that you adopt, because international decision making is still so heavily dominated by the powerful countries.

Whether it is creating the channels of information, determining which decisions have to be made, building up trade and economic pressures, creating political climates, or developing strategic balances—in all these processes, basically the great powers still dominate the world and Third World countries have to develop the methodologies or the instruments to try to keep up with them. That is bound to be their major objective in diplomacy in the future.

9

U.S. DIPLOMACY IN ASIA

U. Alexis Johnson

America's last three wars (World War II, Korea, and Vietnam), which resulted in large part because diplomacy broke down, were started in Asia. Because of this fact and the world influence and economic strength of the Asian nations, particularly Japan and China, Asia will in the future play an even larger role. U.S. diplomacy must be prepared for it.

THE TRADITIONAL ORIENTATION of U.S. diplomacy and academic training must move from its "Eurocentrism" to a better recognition that the center of gravity of the country itself and in its international relations is continuing to move from the east to the west across the Pacific. This seemingly primal thrust immediately asserted itself when, having come west from Europe, the first colonists braved the wilderness to continue the move westward until the continent was conquered. The last census placed the center of our population west of the Mississippi River.

However, our move into the Pacific did not wait for our crossing the continent. Rather, it was initiated by the early New England traders who despatched the *Empress of China* and an American consul to Canton five years before the inauguration of President Washington. Today our trade in the Pacific and with Asia exceeds that with all of Europe.

Along the way, in pursuit of our "manifest destiny," we were very activist (some would say aggressive) in the Pacific and Asia during the many years we were isolationist with respect to the Atlantic and Europe, to the point that we are

now a "Pacific Power" to the degree we have never been an
"Atlantic Power." The Navy established an "Asiatic Squad-
ron" in the 1830s whose "Black Ships" and big guns per-
suaded the Japanese Shogun to open a crack in that country's
isolation. At the same time, in China we were insisting on the
same rights for our traders and missionaries that England had
obtained as a result of the "Opium War." Soon after our Civil
War we bought Alaska from Russia, thus bringing our domain
within three miles of Siberia.

Swallowing our anticolonial professions, we annexed Ha-
waii and eastern Samoa. After "liberating" the Philippines
from Spanish colonial rule, we sent expeditionary forces
seven thousand miles across the Pacific to spend more than
three years in a sanguinary struggle to subdue a Philippine
independence movement. As a consequence of the participation of American troops in 1900 in the allied relief of the
legations in Peking from the "Boxers," American Army and
Marine garrisons were established in Shanghai, Tientsin, and
Peking; and an American Navy river patrol was established
for more than five hundred miles into the heart of China up the
Yangtse River.

With the mediation of President Roosevelt, the treaty end-
ing the 1905 war between Japan and Russia was signed at
Portsmouth, New Hampshire. In 1910, we were the first to
recognize Japan's annexation of Korea. We led the diplomatic
opposition to the Japanese military's thrust into China beginning with the establishment of the puppet state of Manchukuo
in 1931. This policy culminated on our side in July 1941 with
our freezing of Japanese assets, which effectively cut off oil
for the Japanese Navy, and on the Japanese side with the
attack on Pearl Harbor, to be followed only days later by a
German declaration of war against us. Thus, along with the
Korean and Vietnamese wars, it is not improper to say that all
of our last three wars have begun in the Pacific and Asia.

With the largest Soviet fleet now in the Pacific and with the
emphasis on its land and air power, as well as on economic
development, we and our principal adversary are going to
face each other increasingly in this area as well as in Europe.

Thus, with Japan as the second economic power in the world and China as an increasingly stabilized and developing power, the Pacific and Asia are going to be increasingly important to us. We must better recognize this fact in preparing for the future of our diplomacy in that area.

DIPLOMACY IN A CHANGING SOCIETY

Carol C. Laise

We, like other nations, have moved from a diplomacy of compromise to confrontation, largely ignoring in our diplomacy the international institutions set up after the war.

S URVEYING THE DIPLOMATIC landscape from Vermont has some merit because one tends to see things in a larger perspective than is often the case in Washington. I find myself addressing the issues facing the diplomatic service in the context of societal changes rather than from the point of view of managerial problems, which are of a different and less significant order. The main issue, I would like to emphasize, is not attracting outstanding talent to our professional service; it is, as Sam Berger used to say, how to use it more effectively. As I see it, the changes and evolution taking place in the diplomatic arena put, in the words of Secretary Shultz, a "greater premium on consistency, determination and coherence in the conduct of U.S. foreign policy." Yet our system and structure for conducting diplomacy is eroding to a point which some practitioners and commentators characterize as systemic breakdown. In the words of Destler, Gelb, and Lake, we have become "our own worst enemies."

Let us identify some of the important changes that have taken place in the international environment, in the diplomatic process, in the diplomatic functions, and in the diplomatic apparatus. One can deal with the issues of the professional service only in the context of the environment it is designed to serve.

A. Changes in the International Environment

Emerging from the experiences of World War II, in a clearly dominant world position by virtue of our power and resources, and with a domestic national consensus about our role in the world, the United States exercised extraordinary diplomatic leadership in reconciling conflict through agreements and collaborative endeavor: the U.N. Charter, NATO, Marshall Plan, Point Four Program, Arab-Israeli Armistice Agreements, Japanese Treaty, Berlin accords, Limited Test Ban Treaty, ABM and nonproliferation treaties.

Accelerating decolonization, reassertion of nationalism, nuclear stalemate and the resultant diffusion of power, accompanied by clamorous demands of the underprivileged for recognition and a more equitable share of the world's resources, inevitably affected U.S. predominance and, consequently, our diplomatic agenda. As put so succinctly by Henry Kissinger, we found we could no longer overwhelm our problems with our resources. This was amply demonstrated in Vietnam.

As a consequence of the new constraints on its actions, the United States undertook an active diplomacy to compensate for the change in America's relative position and in its diplomatic agenda. We moved to meet the issues of arms control, the changes in the Chinese-Soviet relations, the new opportunities in the Middle East, and festering problems in Latin America. The diplomatic results were: SALT I and II, reopening relations with the People's Republic of China, the Camp David accords on the Middle East, and the Panama Canal Treaties.

More recently, America's response to world problems appears to have shifted—from pursuing our interests through moderating and riding out the disorder in the world to asserting our interests and flexing our muscles to get the world to adjust to the U.S. perspective. No doubt in reaction to the humiliations of Vietnam and Iran, America seems to want to be "number one" again. Curiously enough, however, polls suggest that the price Americans are willing to pay for this is limited. Nationalism is being fanned by ideological prescriptions and the rhetoric of supremacy. The focus is on strength almost to the point of antidiplomacy and confrontation. This has been evident in our dealings with the Soviet Union, in the cases of Grenada and New Zealand, in our handling of the Nicaraguan case in the World Court, and in our unilateral withdrawal from UNESCO. It is worth reflecting on the fact that we have reached very few major international agreements since the founder of the Institute for the Study of Diplomacy, Ellsworth Bunker, completed negotiation of the Panama Canal Treaties in 1977. Many informed people consider it questionable whether we could reach such an agreement in today's climate—let alone achieve congressional ratification.

At this point, it is relevant to note that what is happening seems to be an outgrowth of societal attitudes toward dealing with conflict. When my husband and I returned from Asia in 1973, David Reisman, the noted Harvard sociologist, remarked that one of the major changes in America that had occurred in our absence was that we had become a litigious society, moving from the tradition of compromise toward confrontation in the courts as a way of resolving societal conflicts.

Of course, we are not alone in pursuing our interests through assertive rather than collaborative tactics. Other nations are also pursuing purely nationalistic ends through confrontation rather than diplomacy—the United Kingdom and Argentina over the Falklands, the Soviet Union in Afghanistan, Iran and Iraq, and the tragic case of Lebanon. There is also the new phenomenon of minority groups increasingly resorting to terrorism to achieve their ends. We are confronted with new forms of threats to international order—all the more dangerous in a nuclear age.

Not surprisingly, these trends downgrade the use of the international institutions the United States was instrumental in creating after World War II to help resolve these problems within a diplomatic framework. They are being largely ignored by all of us in varying degrees. Because I was present at the creation of the United Nations at the London preparatory meetings in 1946, worked in its predecessor organization, UNRRA, and also served on U.S. delegations to the U.N. agencies in seven of the early years, I have a keen sense of the gap that has developed between the early vision and present practice.

B. Changes in Diplomatic Process

Last year we celebrated the 200th anniversary of the Treaty of Paris and the role of American diplomacy in achieving our independence. One cannot help but wonder how the changes that have occurred since then in the way we conduct diplomacy have shaped our destiny. Today our diplomatic process has been greatly affected—in some cases for the better, in some for the worse—by a number of interesting phenomena.

With the technological revolution and modern communications, distances have shrunk, time has been telescoped, and diplomatic channels are only one of the many avenues of communication between governments. The media, especially television, have become major players, as evidenced in the case of the Iran hostages. With the emergence of public diplomacy and an explosion in the number of players seeking information, confidentiality in negotiations—without which agreements on serious issues are difficult if not impossible—becomes increasingly problematical.

As the world has become smaller and our basic problems have become global in scale, there has been a proliferation of multilateral institutions such as the International Bank for Reconstruction and Development, the International Monetary Fund, and the Asian Development and Inter-American Development banks, to help orchestrate national monetary and economic policies.

In the United States, as international issues interact more and more with domestic issues, the Congress is demanding a greater role in shaping our diplomatic goals. With the fragmentation of leadership and the pressures exerted by special interests, however, it appears difficult for them to achieve a consensus on the national priorities that should govern our diplomacy. This often results in plenty of criticism and advice, but in insufficient responsible action.

On the executive side of the U.S. government, the presidential preoccupation with managing the politics as well as the substance of foreign policy, along with the awesome responsibility for the nuclear button and other factors, have led to greater concentration of power and decision making on diplomatic issues in the White House staff. This breeds less dependence upon, and even adversarial attitudes toward, the very department whose primary purpose is to present to the president experienced assessments of foreign developments and their impact on U.S. interests. Such centralization in the White House also creates a predisposition toward summitry as a way of resolving diplomatic issues. While there is certainly a role for summitry, the sheer limitations of time and structure at those gatherings act as a constraint on what can be achieved unless they are preceded by extensive preparation and negotiation of the issues at stake through regular diplomatic channels.

The dynamics of these developments lead to a focus and emphasis on gaining short-term national advantages rather than negotiating long-term solutions. Our major problems today are global, and they will only yield to the latter approach. Again, I would observe that this situation has its domestic parallel. In the corporate and financial world, the bottom line seems to be short-term profits, often at the cost of long-term productivity, growth, and gains.

C. Changes in Diplomatic Functions

The traditional diplomatic functions of reporting, interpreting, and negotiating political, security, and economic matters, as well as offering consular services to Americans and foreigners abroad, have now evolved into a far more complex range of activities and subjects. Diplomacy deals with every subject under the sun, from astronauts and arms control to narcotics, telecommunications, and zinc. The pursuit of U.S. interests has led to the establishment of often large operational programs for information and cultural exchange, for economic and military assistance, and for trade promotion. There has thus been a steady expansion of diplomatic functions both quantitatively and qualitatively. Diplomats are called upon to manage complicated negotiations, as well as a vast service enterprise that involves orchestrating official visits and dealing with a wide cross section of the public—business people, artists, media, academia, scientists, and other movers and shakers in our society.

In sum, then, we see that the environment in which today's diplomat is called upon to serve, is indeed a more dangerous place. To pursue our national goals through diplomacy is more important than ever, because a stupid move could destroy us all in a few minutes in the nuclear age. Yet, the climate that fosters confrontation, rather than compromise, short-term political gains over long-term solutions, and complexity rather than clarity in the issues to be resolved, places extraordinary demands on the practitioners of the diplomatic trade. How then is the institution responsible for conducting our diplomacy faring?

D. Changes in the Diplomatic Apparatus

The main instrument for conducting American diplomacy has been the Foreign Service of the United States—a professional career service that has its origins in the Rogers Act of 1924, and whose mission and value to the nation was updated and reaffirmed in the Foreign Service Act of 1980. The Service has grown in size and stature, so that today it numbers 13,000 and provides the core staff for the Department of State, the international programs of other cabinet agencies (Agriculture, Labor and Commerce, AID and USIA, but not CIA) as well as our 152 embassies and missions abroad. It commands respect abroad as one of the ablest diplomatic services in the world; it remains less appreciated at home.

Over the years the Service has undergone democratization, without sacrificing excellence, becoming more representative of the United States, though still short on minorities and women. It has widened its services to Americans abroad, deepened its competence in the new areas of diplomacy, and survived increasing terrorism. What appears to call its role and effectiveness into question today, as a result of the trends I have noted, are several serious developments.

The difference in time frames between the presidential need for immediate results and the tenets of sound diplomacy appears to intensify the pressure to expand politicization of the senior ranks in the Department of State and in embassies. This has consequences affecting the stability of policy and the retention of highly qualified career talent. In this connection, it should be noted that the explosion of knowledge has fostered the phenomenon of think-tank experts, often with agendas of their own, who are finding their way into top policy positions, but who have little practical experience in what will and will not work in reality, and whose limited tenures preclude their being held accountable.

Appointments to these posts appear to attach more value to political loyalty and ideological outlook than to the qualities necessary for successful diplomacy—the personal qualities of tolerance and integrity, the ability to inspire trust and confidence, experience and judgment in relating U.S. interests to the nuances and realities of other cultures, and the ability to communicate effectively. The issue is not career versus noncareer so much as it is the downgrading of professional competence as a requirement for conducting U.S. diplomacy.

Insufficient recognition is given by the Congress and the public to the cost in today's marketplace of attracting, training, and supporting top talent in a worldwide system. Schools such as Georgetown University report that the price of education is forcing top students to seek employment in more lucrative occupations.

The tight constraints on movement, necessitated by security precautions in numerous countries where U.S. diplomats are the targets of terrorism, thwart the purposes and rewards of diplomatic service. Fortresses and security escorts are not conducive to effective communication.

Within the Service itself, societal changes are altering the commitment to service on a worldwide basis and raising very serious questions about whether the diplomatic service can, for long, manage the dual career problem. Career interests of both husbands and wives are factors of increasing importance—in assignments, life style, and retention in the Service. We now have nearly 300 tandem couples working in the Service.

Finally, there are the old refrains relating to lack of guts, low morale, and poor management, but these are chronic, often mistaken, and usually curable depending on the top leadership at State, as the current situation demonstrates. It is true that sorting out structural problems the Foreign Service has made for itself is taking a toll. This is not without remedy, and if properly addressed could become a passing phase.

This litany of developments brings me back to where I began. The evolution of the international system, which has eroded U.S. predominance and has been accompanied by great disorder and danger in the world, puts a greater premium on consistency, determination, and coherence in the conduct of U.S. foreign policy and the performance of U.S. diplomats. Yet, our present domestic system for conducting foreign policy in such a manner seems wide of the mark. The evidence is seen in the wide swings in policy with every change in administration and increasing amateurism in our representation abroad.

We continue on this course at our peril. What appears to be essential is to identify and increase understanding of the causes of this situation. Corrective action will certainly involve greater public support for high professional standards in the practice of diplomacy and a growth in confidence and consensus among leadership groups in the United States about the aims and objectives of U.S. diplomacy.

DIPLOMACY AND THE MEDIA: TWO VIEWS

1 *John Scali*

The media are a powerful force for assisting in the advancement of foreign policy objectives or, if improperly used, for complicating or disrupting them. A proper approach to the media requires sophistication and attention to detail.

I WONDER WHETHER to prepare this paper wearing my former diplomatic hat or the guise in which I spend most of my time in and around the city—that of a reporter who has been in the business approximately forty years. I would like to be as candid as I can because I think this subject is controversial. I believe I have devised a formula. If I write anything that is sensitive to those who are specialists in the diplomatic world, please remember I am writing as a newsman. If I write anything which might upset my news colleagues, remember I am writing in the context of a diplomat.

My subject, the media and diplomacy, is appropriate because at the moment of writing, the media and the government have linked hands to promote and to cover and to tell the world about the historic summit. We have not only Mr. Gorbachev and President Reagan meeting in Geneva, but three thousand reporters as well.

I mention the summit because I think it dramatically illustrates a central fact; that is, that the existence of the media is an indispensable truth of our time which can either mightily assist the advancement of foreign policy objectives or, if improperly used, complicate or disrupt them. I believe that the summit is an example of how the media can assist. The more than month-long barrage of stories about the summit has not occurred because the press and the media decided to inflict cruel and unusual punishment upon the public; but because the government, through deliberate planning, suddenly made available a wide range of speakers of the kind normally tucked in corners, unavailable for discussion until it is time to advance the administration's objectives before the meeting.

Especially noteworthy in this particular case is that no matter how skillfully the administration thought it planned, the Soviet Union planned even more skillfully and with more sophistication and with the kind of attention to detail that has never been a hallmark of Soviet propaganda. Those who keep box scores on what happens even in a presummit environment are prepared to tell you that the Soviets have leaped ahead in the war of words. Their carefully orchestrated campaign of presummit briefings by an official eight-man delegation of image makers, led by Leonid Zamyatin, the head of the Central Committee's International Information Department, has dominated news so far. Along with them, at last count, there were twelve English-speaking Soviet experts in various areas of nuclear disarmament, regional problems, human rights, and other areas of diplomacy. While the United States has continued a measured buildup of publicity, for two weeks most of these gentlemen have been available at the big Geneva press center to greet the early arrivals and to ensure that the initial coverage from Geneva reflected more than a little bit of the Soviet policy.

I find it noteworthy that the Soviets have managed to mount this kind of operation so soon after Mr. Gorbachev has taken office. I think it is deliberately intended as a signal that there is a new, younger, more dynamic, and flexible occupant in the Kremlin who is willing to use all of the modern weapons of diplomacy to make known his goals. Faced with a virtual news blackout by Western spokesmen, the three thousand reporters who are there at this particular time are relying on

Soviet sources for early stories. In addition, they are resorting to a familiar tactic—interviewing themselves. They are also turning to experts they have assembled—academicians, former government officials, former members of Congress, and assorted other experts who are now always instantly available, it seems, whenever they have an opportunity to appear on television at a time when much of the world is watching. It illustrates an awesome truth which has to be considered in any decision about whether to cooperate with, ignore, or fight the press, and that is that sixty-seven percent of the American people say that they rely on television as the major source of their information. I feel sorry for people who reply to pollsters in that way, because to me the written word remains indispensable to discussing a problem in depth.

There is a second that point I would like to make. Although the summit stands out, I think, as an example of how governments can use the media to advance their goals, there are incidents that demonstrate that the press can also be used in a way that is intended to make the achievement of an objective more difficult. I have in mind the letter from Defense Secretary Weinberger to the president, which has been a source of news attention in recent days. I find it very difficult to believe that Defense Secretary Weinberger either leaked that letter or knew that one of his colleagues intended to do so. Mr. Weinberger is a distinguished cabinet officer who has served the nation honorably for many years, and he knows that to leak a letter that seeks publicly to challenge the president on an important issue only hours before he is to meet with the leader of the Soviet government is a grievous sin. It amounts to assisting the opposition to carry out its favorite propaganda tack, namely that the president is dominated by what the Soviets are calling increasingly the "military-industrial rulers" of the United States. I do not know how the *Washington Post* and the *New York Times* succeeded in getting that letter, but I strongly suspect that reporters got the story not because they sought industriously to dig up the information. Rather, as sometimes happens, someone in the government, for reasons of his own, handed it to them to promote a point of view within the government. I cannot say that with any certainty, but as one reporter who has had dozens of pieces of paper handed to him with the same objective in mind, I recognize the telltale marks.

If I had been handed the same letter, I must tell you I would have had a difficult decision to make about whether or not to use it. It demonstrates the extreme measures that some in government would take to embarrass the president of the United States. This happens usually when a zealous advocate of a contrary policy has lost his battle within the government.

I think it is probably going to be very difficult for the *Post* and the *Times* to keep secret who was responsible for leaking the letter. As a former government official, I can only deplore this tactic and say that I find it unforgivable that policy should be influenced by this kind of internecine warfare.

I have been in the news business some forty years. In that period of time, I suspect I have known five hundred important facts about developments which would have merited very important attention in the media. I did not publish one of those because I believed that the government has the right to maintain some information which is of critical secrecy. I do not think that it is the role or the responsibility of the press to publish everything it knows. I think we have to remember that, along with being reporters, we also are citizens of this nation, and that if someone comes to you with information about a Central Intelligence Agency operation to remove Mr. Gadhafi, whether or not one believes the operation or the decision is a wise one, one does not use the information in a news story. Period.

The third point I want to mention is something that Ambassador Samuel Lewis wrote about in *Newsweek*. Ambassador Lewis is a distinguished diplomat who has served his nation ably and well, and whom I have always enjoyed meeting both as a newsman and in my brief career as a government servant. In this particular column, he deplored the need for the State Department to have daily briefings because, he said, these briefings were often the source of on-the-record lectures of other governments that made life more difficult for some ambassadors in certain overseas positions. His recommendation was that to better resist the increasing temptation for the United States government to lecture others, it would be wise just to get rid of the whole institution of daily public briefings. I thought carefully about that and attempted to write something in reply, but decided instead that I would discuss it later, as I am trying to do now.

The problem with Lewis's prescription is that he fails to consider the number of times that that same briefing is used by the State Department to make known carefully written comments that do advance the goals of American foreign policy. I think that for every instance where daily briefings have made life more difficult for X ambassador in Z country, you will find that the use of that forum has been an aid in solving a diplomatic problem. Above and beyond that, I think that one must consider the central purpose for having established daily briefings at the State Department, and that is the need to keep our own American people better informed. Thus, there are several audiences that this forum addresses each day. I think that, as a general prescription, Samuel Lewis's view is one that I cannot accept.

☐2 Dusko Doder

The principal problem for U.S. diplomacy is not the quality of our diplomats and institutions, but obtaining from our national leadership a better sense of purpose and direction. We must devote greater attention to that part of the world beyond Europe and the Soviet Union.

THE FOREIGN SERVICE is one of the best agencies of the U.S. government. In terms of the caliber of people, only the CIA can compare with it. The problem appears to revolve around two principal issues. One is that U.S. policy is subject to numerous domestic pressures which make it difficult to formulate and implement policies that are in the best interest of the country. Another is that of anticipating changes in the world and making advance preparations for them.

George McGhee defines diplomacy as the application of human reason to resolving conflicts. This is true, although the concept is somewhat "rubbery." We do have a good and efficient core of diplomats who know the issues and who know how to implement policies. However, U.S. foreign policy is made not by diplomats, but by politicians, and politicians are subjected to various pressures by U.S. agencies and groups whose knowledge of the outside world may not be as sophisticated as that of the State Department. Such individuals also may be guided by emotion, self-interest, or even ignorance. In chapter 2, Secretary Muskie suggests that we should have public funding for political campaigns as a way to resolve diplomatic difficulties created by various pressure groups. Mr.

Muskie knows the problem, because he was both a United States senator and secretary of state.

The second recommendation, by Jim Billington (chapter 5), addresses the same problem but from a different angle. He would have an administration czar with the authority to inject a greater degree of intelligence and consistency in the application of national policy.

Both of these suggestions were made against the backdrop of Ambassador Laise's presentation (chapter 10) in which she demonstrated the fragmentation of domestic political opinion and the ability of various groups in American society to influence policy. These are, unfortunately, not only ethnic groups. There are other groups with specific interests.

I think one of the most dramatic examples was the coalition that managed to torpedo the SALT II pact. Ambassador David Newsom has an excellent book about it—he was under secretary of state at the time and had an excellent vantage point.[1] The way SALT II was derailed is illuminating. After failing to derail it in congressional debates, the people committed to blocking the ratification of SALT II discovered the emotional issue of Cuba and the so-called Soviet "brigade" in Cuba.

My impression is that the United States has sufficient diplomatic and institutional strength to deal with foreign policy issues, but that difficulties frequently are created by our political leadership, which has to provide a sense of direction and a sense of purpose. Therefore, when we talk about the future, it seems to me that we should not be looking at some marginal problems of the Foreign Service, but rather at the concept of America's role in the world.

We have been preoccupied with the traditional focus of diplomacy—Europe, the Soviet Union, and China—usually ignoring the Third World and the strategic meaning of nationalism in these emerging nations. I think Ambassador Alexis Johnson is absolutely right when he emphasizes the need to

---

[1]*The Soviet Brigade in Cuba: A Study in Political Diplomacy* (Bloomington: Indiana University Press, 1987).

devote greater attention to Asia and the rest of the Third World (chapter 9). The Third World has been at the center of the Cold War for the past four decades—and the theater of active and often bloody struggles—yet none of these has played the triggering role of the Balkans in 1914. The reason for this is, partly, that both the United States and the Soviet Union recognize that their vital interests must not be put to the ultimate test.

Another reason is that nationalism in the emerging world is a powerful force that is likely to preclude the superpowers from acquiring long-term allies there. What we have seen during the past four decades is the inherently limited possibilities for both sides in the Third World, which have led both Moscow and Washington to regard their objectives there as either secondary or negative. As a result, there were no compelling reasons to generate major wars. As we look into the future, however, we can foresee that the ability of the two superpowers to manipulate events in the Third World is bound to decline. Moreover, eventually Third World countries are bound to acquire technological knowhow, and that will require a dramatic adjustment in the world economy. This will be a real challenge for the United States and the West.

The Soviet Union has indicated the change in its own policy by elevating Andrei Gromyko to the presidency. The centrality of Soviet-American relations has been the main preoccupation of Gromyko's life. He always regarded multilateral diplomacy as somehow nonprofessional. He served as foreign minister for twenty-seven years, but never visited an African country, which I think is revealing. The new Soviet leadership sees the future in the context of one world in which Moscow would try to build bridges with all countries. We have already seen some inroads the Russians have made in the Gulf and Southeast Asia.

As a journalist, I want to make one final point. A major problem in shaping and implementing foreign policy is the inability of the government and the press to find a common language. I find John Scali's remarks puzzling and disturbing. If I had five hundred stories, I would most certainly report every single one of them to my editors. However, I would, for instance, argue against the publication of a story about a planned CIA mission into Libya, because I think this is not in the national interest. I think the breakdown of communication, a breakdown of some tacit understanding between the government and the press, is largely a legacy of Watergate. The press is primarily to blame, I believe, however much I hate to admit it. We have gone on a binge in investigating everything and in getting scoops. The government is at fault in trying to hide too much.

What we have today is a curious situation. If I were a government official, I would most certainly not want to talk to a newspaperman; rather, I would let my public relations people handle the press. This is not a healthy state of affairs, and everyone is losing. Foreign governments exploit this situation to weaken the U.S. government's case through the American media; and we as journalists are in the business of reporting news.

When I speak of the need to restore some basic trust between the government and the press, I do not mean that the adversarial aspect of this relationship should be changed. However, both our coverage and our diplomatic performance would benefit from such trust. Let me illustrate this by an example. In 1972, we learned at the *Post* that Soviet Premier Kosygin was involved in a car accident in Moscow. If nothing else, the information illustrated our capacity to monitor the conversations of Soviet leaders over their car telephones. What we did not know was whether Kosygin was seriously incapacitated as a result of the accident. If he was, this obviously was a major story, for it would involve a reshuffle in the Soviet leadership and a new balance of power in the Politburo. If not, it was merely a car accident, not worth reporting if you weighed the fact that the story would compromise our intelligence-gathering facilities. After negotiations with U.S. officials, including some of the top men in the administration, and more reports, we decided not to publish the story, because we trusted officials who told us that they believed Kosygin was not seriously hurt. They turned out to be correct. Today it would be far more difficult to arrange things that way.

DIPLOMACY FOR THE FUTURE

A Summary

George C. McGhee

EAN PETER KROGH has given the following succinct statement on the role of diplomacy: "The Western world is defined by the confidence it places in the utility of diplomacy, which includes negotiation and the willingness to compromise." What are the principal factors that will determine whether diplomacy will in the future perform the useful role that it has proven capable of in the past?

Certainly an important requirement is that our diplomacy be so conducted that the public and our leaders will have confidence in it as an effective instrumentality in maintaining our national security and protecting our interests abroad. Elliot Richardson has pointed out that the State Department has tended to believe that, in addition to being such an instrumentality, it has a certain public constituency of its own, comparable to that attributable to other government departments such as Defense. He considered this a mistake, asserting that the department and its diplomacy exist only as a tool of the president, speaking for the American people, to be used or not as he wished in carrying out policies he chose.

At the end of World War II, our industry was not destroyed as in Europe and elsewhere, but was greatly enhanced. The American people were willing and able to aid devastated countries that desperately sought our help and to fill the world power vacuum. As a result, we engaged in a wide variety of cooperative assistance and defense efforts all around the world and badly needed skillful diplomats to accomplish these tasks. Inevitably, this could not go on forever. The Nixon Doctrine of November 1971 was the first expression of our world retrenchment. The American people had decided that they wanted to do less for the world, and the role of our diplomats had to be adjusted to reflect this general retraction.

The attitudes of various presidents toward the conduct of diplomacy have varied, depending on the relationship between the president and secretary of state. John Kennedy was at first distrustful of the State Department; later, he used it more. The department and its diplomacy could be much more effective if we could get back to the days of Dean Acheson and Harry Truman, who were inseparable in the making of foreign policy decisions.

In recent years, there appears to have been a decrease in the effectiveness of traditional bilateral diplomacy as practiced quietly between foreign offices by professional diplomats. Ambassador Shankar Bajpai of India tells us that the developing countries have tended to see such diplomacy as an extension of the colonial system it helped create. In their desire to achieve their proper influence in the world, which they believe has been denied them, the former colonial nations have resorted more to multilateral diplomacy, particularly in United Nations bodies. Multilateral forums have not, however, turned out to be as effective in their behalf as they had hoped.

According to Ambassador Bajpai, the developing countries, caught between two equally unsatisfactory diplomatic paths, have become disillusioned and are seeking a new framework for diplomacy. If the diplomacy of the future is to fufill its expected role, it must increase the effectiveness of both its bilateral and its multilateral efforts and grant a larger role to the developing nations in the world.

What are the criteria for a successful foreign policy for the future? As Ambassador Bajpai points out, the objective is to influence the decisions of foreign governments. I like Carol Laise's three requirements: coherence, consistency, and continuity. Elliot Richardson emphasizes that diplomacy involves determining the direction of policy, measuring the progress made in achieving goals in that direction, and sticking with it. This means, in our country, that the president must first have an understandable policy that he can persuade the country and Congress to back. A government cannot negotiate if it does not have its own public behind it. Congress is divided into so many competing groups that only a strong president with a clear and coherent policy can pull the many necessary elements together. John Scali points out that the media can be a strong force in the advancement of foreign policy objectives or, if improperly used, for complicating or disrupting them.

This brings out the question of what a policy is. Basically, it is a strategy for using most effectively, through making them self-reinforcing, the limited means a nation has for achieving its foreign policy goals. If you were searching for a child lost in the woods, you would not just wander randomly; you would plan a pattern for the search.

Even a good diplomatic service, if it is to succeed, must have a central intellectual guiding force. The ability to create a successful foreign policy is, I believe, a talent that certain gifted men, like Dean Acheson and Prince Metternich of Austria, obviously possessed. If the diplomacy of the future is to succeed, we must place such men in positions of leadership in the foreign policy process.

Ambassador Laise believes that the principal criterion for our top diplomats is competence, which can be obtained most readily through upgrading the quality of the diplomats we have. We must at the same time, however, provide incentives to attract good career officers, including opportunities for advancement to high diplomatic posts. The morale and effectiveness of our diplomatic service can be impaired by the intrusion of unqualified nonprofessionals into our diplomatic establishment as a reward for political services.

If we are to succeed in our diplomacy, we must understand the changing relationships between nations. Ambassador de Margerie points out that diplomacy with and among the nations that have granted much of their sovereignty to the

Common Market will differ markedly from the bilateral diplomacy of the past. He urges that no diplomatic lines be drawn
to differentiate the developing nations from the industrialized
world, as they were in the past, but that we seek common
points of view with all. Dr. James Billington contends that our
adversarial relationship with the Soviet Union has been the
single most important determinant of U.S. foreign policy
since World War II and will likely remain so until the end of
the century.

Former Senator Edmund Muskie has given, on the basis of
his great experience in public life, a number of requisites for
the successful conduct of diplomacy. The diplomat is like a
politician seeking votes, not for himself but for the nation, in
seeking friends, balancing interests, and occasionally twisting
arms and trading off. This involves hard bargaining, talking,
and compromising. Diplomats must talk with their adversaries
to demonstrate a willingness to hear the other side, clarify
respective positions, and avoid serious misunderstandings in
substance or intentions. Diplomacy requires courage, the
courage to seek solutions to intractable problems, to challenge the conventional wisdom of policies, and to endure the
criticism of those unsympathetic with the process or the
outcome. The job of the diplomat is to find a way that satisfies
the legitimate needs of both sides. We must remain in a
position to play a role in resolving, not exacerbating, local
disputes, and thereby reduce the possibility for Soviet expansion. We should have confidence in our ability to deal with
others. A nation that pulls back from an active role on the
world's diplomatic stage risks losing interests and influence.

Diplomacy must, if it is to succeed in the future, adapt itself
to changing times, including taking advantage of technical
advances in the field of communications and the increased
economic interdependence among the nations. Those who
follow closely developments in diplomacy understand that it
has gone through drastic changes in recent years. Relationships between nations have become less and less the monopoly of the traditional diplomat and increasingly a field for
direct contacts between corporations, scientists, and other

professional and educational groups. Such specialists need little assistance from foreign offices and embassies, which become more and more coordinators and expediters. As Berndt von Staden has written: The distinction between domestic and foreign matters has become blurred. As a result of increased media activity, for example, he believes that little secrecy and little "pure" foreign policy remain. Diplomats cannot change this transformation. If the diplomats of the future are to succeed, they must react to these changes gracefully and make the best of the situation to enhance the effectiveness of their own role.

As John Scali emphasized, our diplomacy will be more effective if we can develop a comprehensive and intelligible overall strategy and enlist the help of the media to communicate it to the American public and Congress. Senator Mathias also notes that we must recognize the specific powers of Congress in the conduct of foreign relations and seek to develop a partnership between the executive branch and the Congress based on accepted common denominators. We must also recognize the legitimate interests of other government agencies. If they are to be successful in the future, the Department of State and our diplomatic corps must, as Elliot Richardson has said, consider themselves participants in the mediation effort required to develop a foreign policy based on a national consensus. This, I believe, can only be accomplished if the result represents the true interests of America as a whole, arrived at through the democratic process and without undue influence by religious, ethnic, business, or partisan political interests.

In the long run, however, I believe that an increased effectiveness in diplomacy can be achieved only if there is an improvement in the world climate in which it operates—if, as Ambassador Bajpai has said, we can recreate the respect that once existed for an international community. We must in the future seek to avoid the injection of uncompromising ideological barriers into the relations between nations. We must be willing to listen to and respect the views and interests of other nations, to negotiate with them with flexibility, and to compromise—always keeping in mind those matters in which we cannot compromise.

As has been pointed out by many observers, a successful strategy in diplomacy relies on many factors other than the substance of the issues involved. The situation within which a negotiation is to be conducted must be made as favorable as possible. This includes certain specifics such as time, place, participants, and agenda. A problem that has proven intractable over a long period of time may suddenly, because of changing circumstances, become "possible." There are few ideas concerning most international problems that have not been thought of. The art of diplomacy is to sense the time at which an idea which has proven nonnegotiable can, because of changes in the many variables involved, be successfully "slipped into place."

The situation that must be created for a successful negotiation must also take into account the political problems of the other government involved, including the particular problems of the head of state. It must be shown that both sides, including one's opponent, can gain from the negotiation. In some instances an avenue of retreat or a "face saver" must be provided if the price is not too great. Skillful use must be made of what is made public and what is kept secret. Where necessary, reliance may have to be placed on agreement by implication—or even innuendo.

It has been said that to succeed, each side to a negotiation must be prepared to survive the failure of a negotiation. This does not necessarily derogate the importance of achieving success in a negotiation. The party who is in the best position to survive a failure is the most likely to succeed in the negotiation.

There has in recent times emerged a defeatist, even cynical, attitude concerning the usefulness of diplomacy. The view is expressed that too much reliance is placed on the success of a negotiation—the agreement or treaty that results—and too little on its workability or subsequent performance under the treaty. It is even said by some that no treaty with communists can be of any value because they cannot be trusted. These are factors that we and other nations must consider, but they should not lead to the conclusion that, for those reasons, we should not try to reach agreement with a communist state, or any other difficult protagonist.

The diplomatic record is replete with examples of successful negotiations with the Soviet Union and other communist states that they have honored. A clever, resourceful diplomat can devise means of assuring compliance by other states with agreements they have entered into. Powerful tools are available through world opinion, sanctions, and pressure exerted by us and in concert with our allies. The refusal on our part to attempt to negotiate because of possible failure or noncompliance represents not so much a reflection on the usefulness of diplomacy, or mistrust of the communists, as a lack of confidence in ourselves.

There are important issues on which the communists are willing to enter into binding agreements entirely on the basis of benefits they perceive, just as we conclude the same agreement based on advantages we see for ourselves. Agreements do not have to represent zero-sum games. They can offer real advantages to both parties. Even the resolution of small differences can prepare the ground for an eventual resolution of greater differences. Even in the absence of full success, the reduction of tension can in itself represent an important advance, while still recognizing that tensions cannot be eliminated without removing their causes.

I oppose very strongly the view of many extremists that reduction of tensions will lull us and the West as a whole into a false sense of complacency, arising from an illusion of a false détente, which will make the status quo so acceptable that longer range goals will be forgotten and central issues will be allowed to remain unresolved. This could be so, but it need not be. A state of heightened tension charges the political atmosphere with fear and suspicion. All prospects that the adversaries will meet each other halfway in a peaceful settlement vanish. Violence or even war could result from artificial challenges that were never part of a basic conflict of vital interests.

I would like to make clear what in my view East-West negotiations are not. They are not an effort calculated merely to produce a favorable attitude on the part of the Soviets—nor a superficial détente unsubstantiated by concrete evidence of progress. They are not based on the vague hope that somehow, if we make unilateral concessions to the Soviets, we will thereby induce in them a feeling of good will or a sense of obligation to make compensatory voluntary concessions to us. The history of our relations with the Soviets provides no basis for assurance that such would be justified.

Yet, even after the ground is narrowed by a prudent skepticism of Soviet intentions, experience has shown that some room for progress still remains. Not all agreements must be based on trust. The most common transaction between individuals all over the world—the exchange of goods over a counter for cash—does not require the element of trust. In East-West relations, the doctrine of caveat emptor must be applied with special care. However, if each party has correctly analyzed the advantages that an agreement offers him, and if, as in the case of a purchase, there is a simultaneous exchange of considerations freely agreed upon, then a basis can be provided for successful agreements—even in the absence of confidence.

History provides little encouragement to believe that major differences between nations can be overcome by peaceful negotiation leading to one massive cataclysmic compromise. Such differences usually persist either until one party succeeds in imposing its will on the other, or the passage of time and the evolution of world affairs so change the international environment that the issues themselves are changed in nature or eliminated.

I do not suggest that we lose either our caution or our sense of values. We must not allow a current of optimism to sweep us into a trap of communist devising. I do believe, however, that our best course is to employ to its fullest capability the time-honored institution of diplomacy, patiently seeking agreements, large and small, which can lead to other agreements. This is infinitely better than creating a situation where two sides draw back from meaningful contact in mutual suspicion, hurling recriminations at each other.

About the Authors

K. SHANKAR BAJPAI was India's ambassador to the United States from 1984 to 1986 and served as consul general in San Francisco, 1967–70. A member of India's career foreign service, he has also been India's envoy in The Hague, Islamabad, and Beijing. His early career was spent in Ankara, Berne, and Karachi, while assignments in the Ministry of External Affairs in New Delhi have included secretary; under secretary, Arab affairs; and deputy secretary, UN Affairs. Ambassador Bajpai is a graduate of Merton College, Oxford, and has also studied at the Ecole des Etudes Universitaires, Geneva. He attended St. Albans School in Washington during the years his father was India's ambassador to the United States.

JAMES H. BILLINGTON is director of the Woodrow Wilson International Center for Scholars, a post he assumed in September 1973. He has taught widely at universities both here and abroad, including Harvard, Princeton, the universities of Leningrad and Puerto Rico, and leading universities in Western Europe and East Asia. He has been visiting research scholar at the Institute of History of the Academy of Sciences of the USSR in Moscow, at the University of Helsinki, and at the Ecole des Hautes Etudes en Sciences Sociales, Paris. He is chairman of the advisory committee of the Georgetown School of Foreign Service graduate program. Dr. Billington is the author of four books, two of which, *The Icon and the Axe* and *Fire in the Minds of Men*, were nominated for National Book Awards. Dr. Billington was valedictorian of the class of 1950 at Princeton and has a Ph.D. from Oxford (1953), where he was a Rhodes scholar at Balliol College.

DUSKO DODER is a veteran foreign correspondent for the *Washington Post*. He was Moscow bureau chief for the *Post* in 1982–85 and served three times as Moscow correspondent, including once with UPI. He has been the *Post* correspondent for Eastern Europe and the Mediterranean, the State Department and Canada and assistant foreign editor. He is the author of *The Yugoslavs* (1978) and *Shadows and Whispers: Power Politics in the Kremlin from Brezhnev to Gorbachev* (1986) and a fellow of the Woodrow Wilson Center at the Smithsonian Institution. Mr. Doder has won the Weintal Prize for Diplomatic Reporting from the Institute for the Study of Diplomacy and an Overseas Press Club Award for Excellence. He has a B.A. from Washington University, St. Louis, and M.A. and M.S. degrees from Columbia University.

U. ALEXIS JOHNSON was U.S. ambassador to Japan (1966–69), Thailand (1958–61), and Czechoslovakia (1953–58), deputy ambassador to Vietnam (1964–65), and U.S. coordinator at the Geneva conference on Indochina and Korea (1954–55). He was under secretary of state for political affairs (1969–73) and chief of the U.S. delegation to the SALT negotiations (1973–77). A career Foreign Service officer for 42 years, he served in Tokyo, Seoul, Tientsin, Mukden, Rio de Janeiro, Manila, and Yokohama, and as deputy director of Northeast Asian affairs and deputy under secretary. He is the author of *The Right Hand of Power* (1984). Among his awards are the Medal of Freedom, the Career Service Award from the National Civil Service League, the Rockefeller Public Service Award, and the President's Distinguished Civilian Service Award. Ambassador Johnson has an A.B. and LL.D. from Occidental College and studied at Georgetown's School of Foreign Service.

CAROL C. LAISE is a former Career Minister in the U.S. Foreign Service who has served as director-general of the Foreign Service, assistant secretary of state for public affairs, and U.S. ambassador to Nepal. She also served in New Delhi and as country director for India, Nepal, Sri Lanka, and the

Maldives, as director of the Office of South Asian Affairs, and in the Bureau of United Nations Affairs. She has served with the U.S. Civil Service Commission and in London with the United Nations Relief and Rehabilitation Administration. She is on the boards of the Institute for the Study of Diplomacy, Phillips Petroleum Company, American Security Bank, Atlantic Council, Mount Holyoke College, Georgetown School of Foreign Service, Experiment in International Living, and Dickinson College. Among her awards are the Federal Woman's Award and the Wilbur Carr Award for Distinguished Service in the Department of State. She has her B.A. and M.A. from American University and honorary LL.D.'s from Windham, Mount Holyoke, Dickinson, and Georgetown University.

EMMANUEL DE MARGERIE is the ambassador of France to the United States. A career diplomat, he has also served as his country's envoy to Spain and the United Kingdom and served previously in Washington as minister-counsellor and in Moscow as first secretary. Assignments have included deputy director in the Ministry of Foreign Affairs, East European section, and director, European Department. Ambassador de Margerie also served as Director of French Museums (1975–77). He is Chevalier, Légion d'honneur; Officier, Ordre Nationale du Mérite; Commdr., Ordre des Arts et des Lettres; and Grand Cross, Order of Isabel la Católica (Spain). He was educated at Aurore University, Shanghai, l'Insitut d'études politiques, Paris, and l'Ecole nationale d'administration.

CHARLES McC. MATHIAS, JR. was U.S. Senator from Maryland from 1968 to his retirement in January 1987. He served on the Foreign Relations, Rules, Judiciary, and Governmental Affairs committees, the Joint Committee on the Library, and the Joint Committee on Printing. Prior to his election to the Senate, he served in the 87th–90th Congresses as representative from the sixth district of Maryland. He has been assistant attorney general of Maryland, city attorney for Frederick, and a member of the Maryland House of Delegates. Senator Mathias received degrees from Haverford College (A.B.) and the University of Maryland (LL.B.) and also studied at Yale University.

GEORGE C. McGHEE served as undersecretary of state for political affairs, U.S. ambassador to the Federal Republic of Germany and to Turkey, State Department counselor, chairman of the State Department's Policy Planning Council, assistant secretary of state, consultant to the National Security Council, ambassador-at-large, coordinator for aid to Greece and Turkey, and senior adviser to the North Atlantic Treaty Council, Ottawa. He is vice-chairman of the board of the Institute for the Study of Diplomacy, has been a director of twelve corporations, and was chairman of the *Saturday Review.* Among the many honors he has received are the Legion of Merit, with three battle stars; Order of Cherifien Empire, Morocco; Distinguished Service Award, U.S. Junior Chamber of Commerce; and honorary citizen, Ankara, Turkey. He is the author of *Envoy to the Middle World* (1983). Ambassador McGhee has degrees from the University of Oklahoma (B.Sc.), Oxford (D. Phil.), where he was a Rhodes Scholar, and four honorary degrees.

EDMUND S. MUSKIE is a senior Washington partner of the firm Chadbourne & Parke and chairman of the board of directors of the Institute for the Study of Diplomacy. He was secretary of state during the latter part of the Carter administration, and a senator from Maine for 22 years beginning in 1958. Earlier, he served as governor of Maine. In 1968 he was the vice presidential candidate of the Democratic Party. Senator Muskie is chairman of the Center for National Policy and serves on the board of the Democrats for the '80s and the Committee for a Responsible Federal Budget. In 1981, he received the Notre Dame Laetare Medal, the Distinguished Service Award from the Association of Former Members of Congress, and the Presidential Medal of Freedom. He is the author of the autobiographical *Journeys* (1972). Senator Muskie has an A.B. cum laude from Bates College, an LL.B. from Cornell, and more than thirty honorary degrees from U.S. colleges and universities.

ELLIOT L. RICHARDSON is the senior resident partner of Milbank, Tweed, Hadley & McCloy. He has served as U.S. secretary of health, education and welfare, secretary of defense, secretary of commerce, and attorney general. He has been U.S. ambassador to the Court of St. James's and special representative of the president to the Law of the Sea conference with the personal rank of ambassador. He has served as lieutenant governor and attorney general of Massachusetts. Among his awards and decorations are the Bronze Star, Purple Heart with oak leaf cluster, the Jefferson Award of the American Institute for Public Service, and the Albert Lasker Special Service Award. He is the author of *Politics and the Individual in America's Third Century* (1976) and numerous other publications. Ambassador Richardson received his degrees from Harvard: A.B. (cum laude), LL.B., and LL.D.

JOHN SCALI is senior correspondent for ABC News, Washington. He began his journalistic career as a reporter with the *Boston Herald*. Other assignments were with the Boston bureau of United Press and with the Associated Press, as a war correspondent and later as diplomatic correspondent in the Washington Bureau. In 1961, he became diplomatic correspondent of ABC News, Washington. He was special counsel to President Nixon for foreign affairs and later U.S. ambassador to the United Nations (1973–75). He has received the Journalism Award from the University of Southern California and special awards from the Washington chapter of the National Academy of Arts and Sciences and the Overseas Press Club. A John Scali award has been created by the Washington chapter of the American Federation of Television and Radio Artists. Ambassador Scali has a B.S. degree in journalism from Boston University.

BERNDT von STADEN, a career officer in the West German foreign service, was ambassador to the United States in 1973–79. Earlier, he served in Washington as counsellor of embassy and twice in Brussels. Assignments in the Ministry of Foreign Affairs in Bonn have included director of Soviet Affairs, deputy assistant state secretary, assistant state secretary, head of the Political Department, and state secretary of the Foreign Office. In 1985, he was William Fulbright Distinguished Research Professor of Diplomacy at the Georgetown University School of Foreign Service and is to teach there again in 1987. Immediately prior to joining the faculty at Georgetown, Ambassador von Staden was coordinator for German-American cooperation in the field of inter-social relations, cultural and information policy. He was educated at Bonn and Hamburg universities and has been awarded his country's Order of Merit.